AN INTRODUCTION TO LUTHERAN TEACHING

D.T. Strelan

Lutheran Publishing House

GOD FOR US

Copyright © 1988 Lutheran Publishing House, Adelaide, South Australia. All rights reserved. No part of this book may be reproduced in any manner (except for brief quotations embodied in articles or reviews) without the expressed written permission of the publisher.

Bible quotations, unless otherwise indicated, are from *The Holy Bible, New International Version*, © 1978 New York International Bible Society, and are used by permission of Zondervan Bible Publishers.

Graphic Design: Graeme Cogdell

First printing March 1988
Second printing April 1988
Third printing January 1989

National Library of Australia
Cataloguing-in-Publication data

Strelan, David, 1934–
   God for us.

   ISBN 0 85910 430 3

   1. Lutheran Church — Doctrines. 2. Christian life.
   I. Title.

248.4'841

Printed and published by
Lutheran Publishing House
205 Halifax Street, Adelaide, South Australia

LPH 1805-88

A FIRST WORD

This book has been written in response to repeated requests from pastors and lay people for a presentation of the basic Bible truths in non-technical language and an attractive format.

The title of the book comes from one of the great chapters of the Bible: Romans 8 — in particular, v 31: 'If God is for us, who can be against us?' God is for us in his Son Jesus. God is for us in life, in death, and for eternity. God is for us, and nothing can separate us from his undeserved love. *God For Us* takes us to the heart of the Bible and of Lutheran teaching.

God For Us has been prepared as a resource for use in adult pre-membership classes. It is not an exhaustive treatment, but it does cover the main teachings of the Lutheran Church, and will enable 'inquirers' to make their decision about membership in this church. Pastors and other class-leaders will naturally want to ensure that there are follow-up opportunities for growth after the use of this course.

As well, this book is offered as a 'refresher course' for people who already belong to the church. *God For Us* is commended for the study of the basics of the Christian faith in small groups or by private reading.

Martin Luther's great discovery from the Bible was that God is not a fierce tyrant who is against us because we fail to meet his demands, but is a loving Father who is for us, who forgives and accepts us in mercy for Jesus' sake. Of his discovery of this truth, Luther wrote: 'I felt myself to be reborn and to have gone through open doors into paradise. The whole Bible took on a new meaning.'

May that loving God grant a similar experience to many who read and study this book.

Epiphany 1988 **David Strelan**

CONTENTS

1. For Non-Achievers Only 5
2. Amazing Grace 11
3. 'But How Do We Know?' 17
4. He's Got the Whole World in His Hands 22
5. Baptism: God Is For Me! 26
6. Power for Living 30
7. God For Us — For Sure! 34
8. We Are the Church 39
9. Full-time Christianity 43
10. God For Us — For Ever 48

Appendixes:
    Ready Reference 53
    The Church Year 60
    A Look at Liturgy 61
    A Brief Historical Background 63

FOR NON-ACHIEVERS ONLY   1

WHAT DECIDES whether or not a person is valued and respected in our society? Look through the following list. Which of these people are usually rated highly in our society? Which would get the lowest rating?

- doctors
- scientists
- unemployed
- handicapped
- drug-pushers
- politicians
- child-abusers
- businessperson
- old people
- sports stars
- clergy

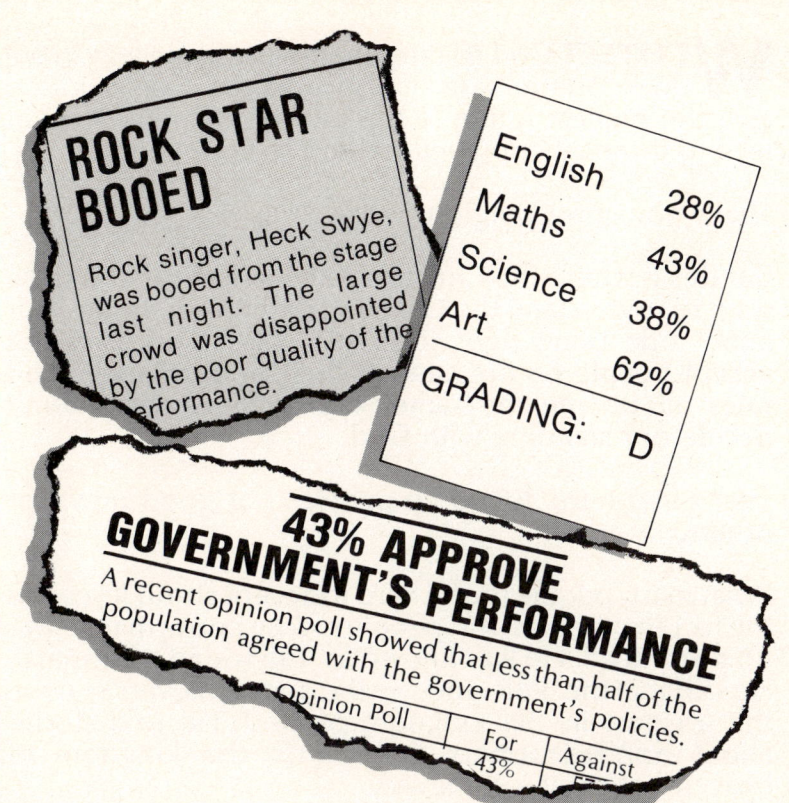

NOTES

SOCIETY puts a lot of emphasis on performance and achievement. If I want to be accepted, I have to perform. I am judged according to my performance at work, at school, at home, in my marriage and family, even at church.

Society tends to push aside those people who cannot or do not perform.

So we spend our lives trying to prove ourselves, to show by our performance that we are as good as the next person, or even better! We want people to see that we measure up. And if we put in the performance, we expect to get the recognition. That's only fair! It's the rule we live by. It's what we believe in. It's our religion.

Our religion? Does God fit into this pattern?
Is that the way God acts?

LOOK AGAIN through the list on the previous page. How would God rate the people on that list? Which two might get the highest rating from God? Which two might rate lowest?

We cannot ever perform well enough ...

WE EXPECT God to rate people the same way as we do — on the basis of performance. God ought to give the highest rating to the best performers — or at least to those who try their hardest to do the right thing.

That's how most religions work.

But this is where the Christian religion is different. If we want to understand the Christian faith, we must be clear about one thing right from the start: **God does not accept people on the basis of their performance. God rates all people the same. Our achievements don't decide our standing with God.**

That's bad news for some people, but good news for others.

What many people found hard to accept about Jesus was the fact that he was 'for' people whose performance was no good at all. He was known as 'the friend of sinners'. He said that the 'little ones' — the non-achievers — were the greatest in the kingdom of God. He told stories about non-performers going into the kingdom of heaven before the achievers.

God is really **'for us'**, Jesus said. But this is not because of our performance. It cannot be because of who we are or what we have done.

Why not?

Because we do not, and we cannot, ever perform well enough to meet the standard God sets and expects of us.

BIBLE SEARCH

READ **LUKE 18:9-14**

What was surprising about God's judgment of these two men?

For what kind of people is this story bad news?

For whom is this story good news?

NOTES

PAGE 6

TEST YOURSELF OUT!

THINK ABOUT your relationship with other people. What's your performance like?

The performance God expects from every one of us is set down quite clearly in the Bible:
'Love your neighbour as yourself!' (Mark 12:31)

('Neighbour' = every other person; 'love' = giving ourselves for the good of others.)

TALK ABOUT what other people expect of us and what we expect of them. How do we measure up to the expectations of our marriage partner, or friends, or children, or bosses, etc?

	What God expects	Our performance
As parent	100% love	____%
As husband/wife	100% love	____%
As neighbour	100% love	____%
As citizen	100% love	____%
As employer/employee	100% love	____%
In our words	100% love	____%
In our thoughts	100% love	____%
In our actions	100% love	____%

If God is **'for'** only those people whose performance measures up to what he expects, we won't get on very well, will we?

But there's another test.

God also commands: **'Love the Lord your God with all your heart and with all your soul and with all your mind and with all your strength'** (Mark 12:30).

This is the **'most important'** commandment, Jesus said. It sums up everything God expects from us and demands of us. All the Ten Commandments flow from this one.

What God Expects
100% love for him

Our Performance
____%
The pass-mark in God's test is 100%! Even 99.9% is failure. The Bible says: **'Whoever keeps the whole law and yet stumbles at just one point is guilty of breaking all of it'** (James 2:10). How, then, can we ever imagine that God ought to be 'for us' because of our good performance?

PAGE 7

BIBLE SEARCH

READ **ROMANS 3:10–12,23**

Is this an accurate description of human beings? Do you know anyone to whom these statements do not apply?

Discuss this statement: 'If God is for any one, he must surely be for those people who at least try to do the right thing'.

N O T E S

WHAT'S THE PROBLEM?

Why can't we live up to what God expects?
Why can't our performance measure up?

There's something basically wrong with us. There's something wrong with human nature, the way it is now. It's natural for us to go against God, to break his laws by our thoughts, wishes, words, and actions.

If God were to deal with us on the basis of our performance, then he would surely be **against** us — totally! If we were to get what we deserve, that would mean only anger, rejection, punishment, death.

But God is for us! He loves us. He has forgiven us. This good news is the centre of the Christian faith.

How can this be possible?

THE TEN COMMANDMENTS

The Ten Commandments are God's good gifts intended for the protection and happiness of his creatures. They spell out some of the details of what it means both to love God (commandments 1–3 in particular) and to love our neighbour (4–10). They apply to every part of our lives — not only actions, but also attitudes, feelings, wishes, words.

Because we can't keep the Commandments perfectly, they offer no grounds for hoping that God will be 'for us'.

The Commandments accuse and condemn us as sinners who need God's mercy.

 **THE CHURCH TEACHES**
in Luther's *Small Catechism*

The Ten Commandments
I am the Lord your God.

1 THE FIRST COMMANDMENT
You shall have no other gods.
What does this mean for us?
We are to fear, love, and trust God above anything else.

PAGE 8

KEY BIBLE STATEMENTS

- Be holy because I, the Lord your God, am holy.
(Leviticus 19:2)

- If we claim to be without sin, we deceive ourselves and the truth is not in us. If we confess our sins, he is faithful and just and will forgive us our sins and purify us from all unrighteousness.
(1 John 1:8,9)

- Through the law we become conscious of sin.
(Romans 3:20)

- Love is the fulfilment of the law.
(Romans 13:10)

- All who rely on observing the law are under a curse, for it is written: 'Cursed is everyone who does not continue to do everything written in the Book of the Law'.
(Galatians 3:10)

2 THE SECOND COMMANDMENT
You shall not take the name of the Lord your God in vain.
What does this mean for us?
We are to fear and love God so that we do not use his name superstitiously, or use it to curse, swear, lie, or deceive, but call on him in prayer, praise, and thanksgiving.

3 THE THIRD COMMANDMENT
Remember the Sabbath day, to keep it holy.*
What does this mean for us?
We are to fear and love God so that we do not neglect his Word and the preaching of it, but regard it as holy and gladly hear and learn it.

*Some prefer the translation: 'You shall sanctify the holy day'.

4 THE FOURTH COMMANDMENT
Honour your father and your mother.
What does this mean for us?
We are to fear and love God so that we do not despise or anger our parents and others in authority, but respect, obey, love, and serve them.

5 THE FIFTH COMMANDMENT
You shall not kill.
What does this mean for us?
We are to fear and love God so that we do not hurt our neighbour in any way, but help him in all his physical needs.

6 THE SIXTH COMMANDMENT
You shall not commit adultery.
What does this mean for us?
We are to fear and love God so that in matters of sex our words and conduct are pure and honourable, and husband and wife love and respect each other.

7 THE SEVENTH COMMANDMENT
You shall not steal.
What does this mean for us?
We are to fear and love God so that we do not take our neighbour's money or property, or get them in any dishonest way, but help him to improve and protect his property and means of making a living.

8 THE EIGHTH COMMANDMENT
You shall not bear false witness against your neighbour.
What does this mean for us?
We are to fear and love God so that we do not betray, slander, or lie about our neighbour, but defend him, speak well of him, and explain his actions in the kindest way.

9 THE NINTH COMMANDMENT
You shall not covet your neighbour's house.
What does this mean for us?
We are to fear and love God so that we do not desire to get our neighbour's possessions by scheming, or by pretending to have a right to them, but always help him keep what is his.

NOTES

10 THE TENTH COMMANDMENT

You shall not covet your neighbour's wife, or his manservant, or his maidservant, or his cattle, or anything that is your neighbour's.

What does this mean for us?

We are to fear and love God so that we do not tempt or coax away from our neighbour his wife or his workers, but encourage them to remain loyal.

WHAT DOES GOD SAY OF ALL THESE COMMANDMENTS?
He says:

'I, the Lord your God, am a jealous God, visiting the iniquity of the fathers upon the children to the third and fourth generation of those who hate me, but showing steadfast love to thousands of those who love me and keep my commandments.'

What does this mean for us?

God warns that he will punish all who break these commandments. Therefore we are to fear his wrath and not disobey him. But he promises grace and every blessing to all who keep these commandments. Therefore we are to love and trust him, and gladly do what he commands.

MORE TO THINK ABOUT

1 Think about what this chapter is saying to you personally about God and yourself. Does this chapter call for any changes in your
. . . beliefs?
. . . attitudes?
. . . conduct?
. . . lifestyle?

2 Try your hardest every day for the next week to keep all the Ten Commandments perfectly. At the close of each day, check back over the day's performance. Which commandment(s) do you find hardest to keep? Ask God to forgive your sins especially against that commandment (or those commandments).

3 Read the following Bible passages, and in each instance pinpoint what kind of people God accepts:
Matthew 20:1–16; Luke 14:16–24; Matthew 5:1–16; Matthew 9:9–13; Matthew 18:1–4.
Now write a short statement beginning: 'From these Bible passages, I learn that God . . .'

AMAZING GRACE **2**

I love you.

I love you when . . .

I love you because . . .

I love you, but . . .

I love you, even though . . .

What kind of limits or conditions do we put on our love? What would make us stop loving someone?

Which of these I-love-you statements sounds most like unconditional, undeserved love?

GOD LOVES US — that is, God loves all people. And when he says: 'I love you', there are no ifs or buts. He loves us without any conditions, with no strings attached.

God is totally 'for us'. He always has been, and he always will be. He loves us so much that he wants us to share life with him — starting now, and going on for ever. And he offers each one of us this everlasting life as a gift: We don't have to work for it, we don't have to pay for it.

God's love for us has nothing to do with what kind of people we are or try to be. It does not depend on how well we have behaved or performed.

In fact, God loves us *even though* we have not loved him, *even though* we deserve that he should be angry with us because of our disobedience. Could we blame him if he had turned his back on us completely?

Instead, God comes to us with open arms. His love is undeserved and unlimited.

It is amazing grace.

THE GREATEST GIFT

God does not just *say* that he loves all people; he *proves* this by meeting our needs. He gave us our beautiful world because he loves us. For the same reason he looks after us, giving us food and protection.

But God's greatest gift of undeserved love is Jesus Christ, his only Son. The Bible says: **'God so loved the world that he gave his one and only Son, that whoever believes in him shall not perish but have eternal life'** (John 3:16). God's love is not just nice words and warm feelings; it is giving and acting **for us**.

About 2000 years ago God proved once and for all that he is 'for us' by sending his Son to earth to attend to our greatest need: to bring all people back into a right relationship with him.

BIBLE SEARCH

READ **MATTHEW 18:23–27**

What do you find in this story that is not like real life?

How are we supposed to see ourselves in this story?

NOTES

THE STORY OF JESUS

'The strangest person who ever lived' is one way of describing Jesus Christ. There has never been anyone like him. Throughout his life, people were faced with the question: Who is this man? That is a question we still face today as we read the Bible account.

LUKE 1:26–38
LUKE 2:1–20
MATTHEW 2:1–12

From the very beginning there is something strange about Jesus. When his mother is pregnant with him, she says that she is still a virgin! Strange things happen when he is born in a stable. Shepherds and wise men who come to visit him call him 'Christ, the Lord' ('Lord' was God's name in the Old Testament) and 'King of the Jews'.

MATTHEW 3:13–17

But then nothing much is heard of Jesus for 30 years, until he is baptized, and the time comes for him to begin his work. At his baptism a strange voice is heard, saying: 'This is my own dear Son'.

The Son of God? Is that who he is?

JOHN 7:40–49

Jesus begins to preach and teach. He talks about God as his Father. Crowds flock to him, because he seems to know what he is talking about. 'No one ever spoke like this man', they say.

MATTHEW 9

And his word has power — special power to control nature and to change people's lives. When he speaks, sick people get better, blind people see, lame people walk. Even a few dead people become alive again.

When he comes to some people and says: 'Follow me', they obey — just like that! There is something about him that attracts them. And as they follow and listen and watch, they notice two distinct sides to him. On the one hand, they see power and authority and glimpses of sheer glory; on the other hand, the same Jesus seems so frail and totally human. One minute, he breaks down and cries because his good friend has died; the next, he commands the dead man to come out of the grave, and it happens.

MATTHEW 8:23–27
JOHN 11

MATTHEW 16:13–20

Who is he? The crowds think he is a prophet. His disciples say: 'You are the Christ, the Son of the living God.' But the religious leaders find another answer: His power is from the devil, they

God (circle) was born as a lowly baby (manger) to be our Saviour (ihc) and King (crown).

By his perfect sacrifice for sin (lamb) on the cross, Jesus has defeated sin, death, and the devil for us (banner).

An ancient symbol for Jesus. The letters of the Greek word for 'fish' stand for 'Jesus Christ, God's Son, Saviour'.

say. If he has any sort of connection with God, why does he mix with 'sinners' and not give 'good' people their proper recognition? Why doesn't he judge people on their merits?

MATTHEW 21:1-9

Jesus' ministry comes to an end after about three years. The crowds cheer him into Jerusalem as 'King of the Jews'; they imagine that he will now drive out the Roman occupation forces. But nothing happens — he simply teaches in the temple. The crowd's mood changes.

MATTHEW 21-25

MATTHEW 26

Meanwhile, Judas makes a deal with Jesus' enemies to betray him. Jesus is captured without a struggle. The leaders put him on trial before their council. They find him guilty of blasphemy because of his claim to be the Christ, the Son of God.

MATTHEW 27

They drag Jesus off to Pontius Pilate, the Roman governor, to have their death sentence confirmed. Pilate wants to know who Jesus is. 'Are you the King of the Jews?' he asks. Though he finds Jesus not guilty of any crime, under pressure from the crowd he sentences him to be crucified.

Jesus is nailed to a cross like a criminal, even though he has never done a single wrong thing. The people mock him: 'If you are the Son of God, come down!' He suffers extreme agony. He goes through hell, totally abandoned even by his Father. He dies. And the Roman captain says: 'Truly this man was the Son of God!'

MATTHEW 27:54

Jesus' body is placed in a grave.

MATTHEW 28

About 36 hours later, some women, who come to the grave to anoint Jesus' body, find that the grave is empty. Jesus appears to them and to some of his followers. Again they face the question: 'Who is he?' He finally convinces them that he is alive again. Even doubting Thomas now calls him 'my Lord and my God!'

JOHN 20:28

ACTS 1:1-11

In the next 40 days, Jesus appears to his disciples on several occasions. He explains to them that his death and resurrection had to happen because this is how God planned to save the world from sin and death. He gives them instructions to preach this good news to all people. Before he leaves them and goes back to his Father, he promises to send the Holy Spirit to answer fully all their questions about who he is and why he came.

JOHN 14:26

BIBLE SEARCH

READ **ACTS 10:34-43**

This is a summary of Jesus' life and work.
Which name of God is used for Jesus? (v 36)

What works does Jesus do that only God can do? (vv 38, 41, 42, 43)

Why did the Son of God become a human being?

NOTES

WHO IS JESUS CHRIST?

'The best person who ever lived' . . . 'a great teacher' . . . 'a perfect example for us to follow' . . . 'a great hero who died for what he believed in': these are some of the things people say about Jesus today.

It sounds great! But it is not enough.

Jesus claimed to be **the Son of God, true God,** equal with his Father. 'I and the Father are one', he said (John 10:30). *Either* his claim is true and must be accepted with all its implications, *or* Jesus is a liar or a lunatic, whose claim must be totally rejected. There is no other possibility.

Christians believe that Jesus Christ has always existed as true God together with his Father and the Holy Spirit. But in order to rescue the human race from sin, death, and hell, he also became true man.

FOR US . . FOR OUR SALVATION

Why did God lower himself and become a human being? Why did he live such a lowly life, and die such a shameful death? And how does all this show God's amazing grace to us today?

Jesus came **for us**, for every human being. He took our place.

He was born **for us**, to make up for our sinful birth. He lived a perfect life **for us**, to make up for our terrible performance.

Jesus took our sins on himself. He took the blame for our disobedience. He suffered **for us**. He died **for us**. He went through hell **for us**.

But Jesus also won the victory over sin, death, and the devil **for us**. He rose again **for us**, to break the power of death over us. He ascended into heaven to prepare a place **for us**. As our living Lord, he is with us always, and rules all things **for us**.

Jesus died and rose again for us.

BIBLE SEARCH

READ **JOHN 20:30,31**

What is your answer to the question: 'Who is Jesus Christ?'

NOTES

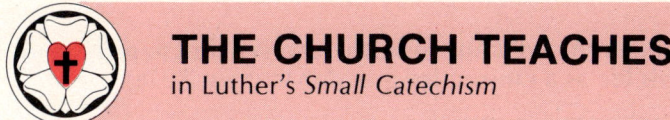

THE CHURCH TEACHES
in Luther's *Small Catechism*

(From the Apostles' Creed)

I believe . . . in Jesus Christ, his only Son, our Lord; who was conceived by the Holy Spirit, born of the Virgin Mary, suffered under Pontius Pilate, was crucified, dead and buried; he descended into hell; the third day he rose again from the dead; he ascended into heaven, and sits at the right hand of God, the Father Almighty; from thence he will come to judge the living and the dead.

WHAT DOES THIS MEAN?

I believe that Jesus Christ — true God, Son of the Father from eternity, and true man, born of the Virgin Mary — is my Lord. At great cost he has saved and redeemed me, a lost and condemned person. He has freed me from sin, death, and the power of the devil — not with silver or gold, but with his holy and precious blood and his innocent suffering and death. All this he has done that I may be his own, live under him in his kingdom, and serve him in everlasting righteousness, innocence, and blessedness, just as he is risen from the dead and lives and rules eternally. This is most certainly true.

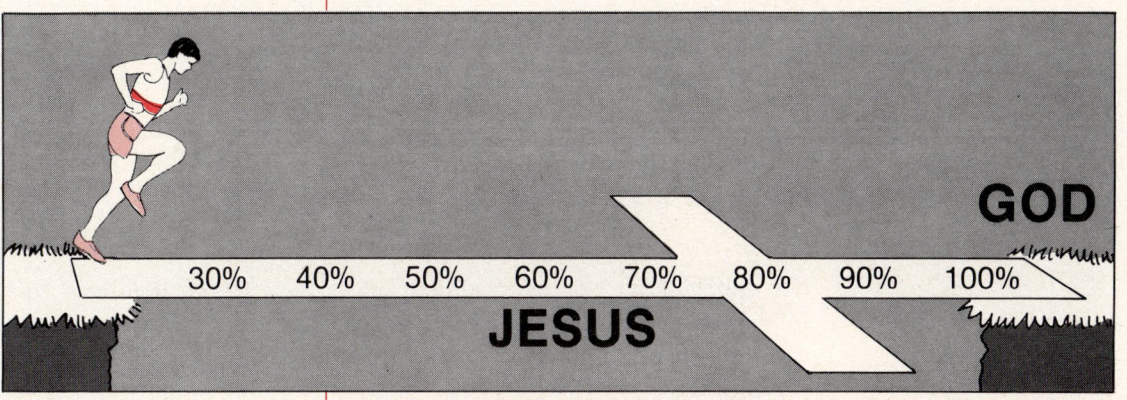

THE BIBLE SAYS

Here are some Bible statements in which Jesus explains why he came to earth:

- 'I have . . . come to fulfil [the law and the prophets]' (Matthew 5:17).

- 'I did not come to judge the world, but to save it' (John 12:47).

- 'I have come that they may have life, and have it to the full. I am the good shepherd. The good shepherd lays down his life for the sheep' (John 10:10,11).

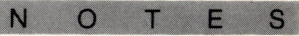

NOTES

BIBLE SEARCH

READ **ROMANS 3:20–28**

Why can't you be 'righteous in his sight' by doing good works?

How do you become right with God or 'not guilty' in his sight?

KEY BIBLE STATEMENTS

- God so loved the world that he gave his one and only Son, that whoever believes in him shall not perish but have eternal life. (John 3:16)

- It is by grace you have been saved, through faith — and this not from yourselves, it is the gift of God — not by works, so that no one can boast. (Ephesians 2:8,9)

- [Jesus said:] I am the way and the truth and the life. No one comes to the Father except through me. (John 14:6)

- God demonstrates his own love for us in this: While we were still sinners, Christ died for us. (Romans 5:8)

- Look, the Lamb of God, who takes away the sin of the world! (John 1:29)

- [Jesus said:] Before Abraham was born, I am! (John 8:58)

- 'The Son of Man did not come to be served, but to serve, and to give his life as a ransom for many' (Matthew 20:28).

- 'This is what is written: The Christ will suffer and rise from the dead on the third day, and repentance and forgiveness of sins will be preached in his name to all nations' (Luke 24:46,47).

FORGIVEN — BY GRACE THROUGH FAITH

We could never make up for the wrong we have done. But God has shown us grace (undeserved love). Because Jesus took the blame and punishment for the sins of the world, God has declared all people forgiven **for Jesus' sake**, and offers this forgiveness as a free gift to all.

Everyone who trusts in Jesus as the Saviour has the forgiveness of all sins. Every believer in Jesus can say with complete confidence: 'God is **for me**!'

The Bible says: **'There is no difference, for all have sinned and fall short of the glory of God, and are justified freely by his grace through the redemption that came by Christ Jesus'** (Romans 3:22-24).

God has declared us 'not guilty'. He has pronounced us innocent, or 'righteous'. He has 'justified' us.

'Justification by grace' is the central teaching of the Christian religion. God is **for us**, not because of our performance or 'good works'; but he justifies us
- **by grace**
- **for Christ's sake**
- **through faith.**

MORE TO THINK ABOUT

1 Think about what this chapter is saying to you personally about God and yourself. Does this chapter call for any changes in your …beliefs? …attitudes? …conduct? …lifestyle?

2 Begin reading the story of Jesus in one of the gospels (Matthew, Mark, Luke, or John). Plan to read at least a chapter a day. Look for answers to two main questions: *Who is Jesus Christ?* and: *Why is Jesus important to your life?*

3 Check the following Bible statements about Jesus:
Isaiah 53: A prophecy about Jesus.
John 1:1-14: Jesus is 'the Word'.
Acts 1:1-11: Jesus goes back to heaven.
1 Corinthians 15:1-23: The resurrection of Jesus is the centre of our faith.
Philippians 2:5-11: Jesus humbled himself to save us.

'BUT HOW DO WE KNOW?'

3

HOW do we know:

...who discovered our country?

...whether or not someone loves us?

...that nuclear war could destroy civilization?

IS GOD REAL?

HOW DO we *know* God is for us?

How do we *know* that God even exists?

If there is a God, how do we *know* who he is and what he is like? How do we get to know him as *our* God?

All people seem to have a built-in idea that there is some kind of God. For example, our conscience might tell us that there is a higher authority to whom we have to answer. Or the beauty and order of our marvellous universe might raise the question: Is there a Creator? Or things happen in our lives which make us wonder whether there isn't some higher power controlling our destiny.

This instinctive, *'natural'* knowledge of God is too limited to be of much use. It doesn't tell us who God is. It leaves us guessing at, or trying to work out, our own idea of God — which helps to explain why there are so many different religions in the world.

The natural knowledge of God doesn't answer the really big question: Is God for us or against us?

JESUS IS THE ANSWER

We can know that there is a God, and who God is, because God has introduced himself personally through Jesus. Jesus Christ is God's way of saying: 'I am real. And I love you. I am God for you.'

Jesus is **God's revelation of himself**. If we want to know God, we look at Jesus. If we want to know what kind of being God is, we look at Jesus. His words and works show us the truth about God: he is almighty, all-knowing, all-wise, everlasting, present everywhere. He is not limited by space or time or physical laws, as we are.

The most important truths Jesus shows us about God are that he is perfect and right in everything he does, and that his love is perfect.

BIBLE SEARCH

READ **HEBREWS 1:1,2** and **JOHN 1:1–14**

What, according to the Bible, is the clearest way in which God has made himself known?

John calls Jesus 'The Word'. Why is this a good name for him?

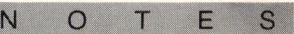

NOTES

PAGE 17

'THE BIBLE TELLS ME SO'

But we can't see Jesus. How do we know that he is real?

We find out about Jesus from the Bible. Jesus is the great central character in this unique book. The Old Testament has the promise that the Messiah, or Christ, would come. The New Testament tells how this promise came true in the coming of Jesus. Jesus himself said: 'The Scriptures testify about me' (John 5:39).

The Bible is God's *written* revelation. It is God's Word in human words, written by many different people over many centuries. God inspired men to write his Word in their own style and language.

Everything we need to know about God is in the Bible.

THE ONE TRUE GOD

The Bible tells us there is only **one** God. All other 'gods' are human inventions.

The only true God is the God who made heaven and earth, the God who became man for us in the person of Jesus Christ, the God who calls and leads people into a right relationship with himself.

The one true God is three separate, distinct Persons in one Being:

- **The Father,** who created all things;
- **The Son,** who became a human being to save the world;
- **The Holy Spirit,** who brings people to faith in Christ, and makes them the holy people of God.

Each Person — Father, Son, and Holy Spirit — is true God. Yet there are not three Gods, but only one. Christians use the term 'triune' (three-in-one) to describe God.

God is so much greater than we are that it is not surprising that we can't understand the mystery of his being. God does not ask us to understand; he invites us to believe, to trust what his Word tells us.

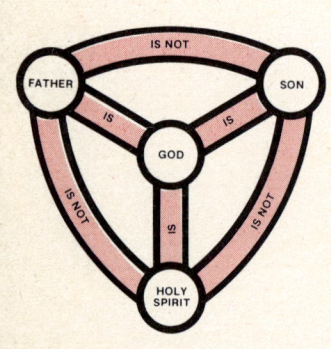

READ **2 TIMOTHY 3:15–17**

What help can we get from reading the Bible?

In what way is 'all Scripture' different from other writings?

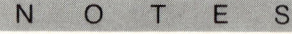

N O T E S

God creates, blesses, promises, gives, forgives

People disobey, sin, bring punishment on themselves

TWO MAIN THEMES

There are two main themes in the Bible:

- The **grace** of God
- The **sin** of human beings

These themes are repeated over and over again. They come together especially in Jesus' life, death, and resurrection.

TWO MAIN MESSAGES

There are two main messages from God which the Bible communicates: the **Law** and the **Gospel**.
These two messages are very different from each other. We need to hear both, and to apply them to ourselves.

THE LAW	THE GOSPEL (Good News)
...tells us what God wants us to do and not to do, and what kind of people God wants us to be;	...tells us what God has done for us in love;
...shows us our sins;	...shows us our Saviour;
...shows us God's anger;	...shows us God's grace;
...demands, warns, condemns, punishes, makes us slaves.	...promises, offers, gives, forgives, saves, sets us free.

Recognizing and understanding Law messages and Gospel messages helps us understand the Bible better.

FOR EXAMPLE:

An example of a Law message and a Gospel message in one Bible verse:

'The wages of sin is death, but the gift of God is eternal life in Christ Jesus our Lord.' (Romans 6:23)

BIBLE SEARCH

READ **MATTHEW 22:1-14**

This is a parable about God and his people. What does it say about the grace of God and about the sin of human beings?

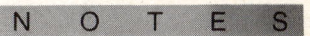

N O T E S

KEY BIBLE STATEMENTS

- The holy Scriptures... are able to make you wise for salvation through faith in Christ Jesus. (2 Timothy 3:15)

- All Scripture is God-breathed and is useful for teaching, rebuking, correcting, and training in righteousness. (2 Timothy 3:16)

- [Jesus said:] Blessed... are those who hear the word of God and obey it. (Luke 11:28)

- Now this is eternal life: that they may know you, the only true God, and Jesus Christ, whom you have sent. (John 17:3)

- May the grace of the Lord Jesus Christ, and the love of God, and the fellowship of the Holy Spirit be with you all. (2 Corinthians 13:14)

- Faith comes from hearing the message, and the message is heard through the word of Christ. (Romans 10:17)

- No one can say 'Jesus is Lord', except by the Holy Spirit. (1 Corinthians 12:3)

A MATTER OF FAITH

But how do we know the Bible is true? How do we know Jesus is real? Is there any proof?

In the long run, this is a matter of **faith.** Faith means taking God at his Word, without proof. It means trusting Jesus and accepting the Bible as true, even when we don't see any evidence, even when we can't understand.

Christian faith does not come naturally to us. It is the special gift of the Holy Spirit. Whenever we read or hear God's Word, the Spirit is at work, teaching us to believe what God tells us.

- The Holy Spirit uses the **Law of God** to show us our sin and our need of a Saviour.

- The Holy Spirit uses **the Gospel** to show us our Saviour. He teaches us to believe in and trust Jesus, through whom God is for us.

- The Holy Spirit leads us into **all truth** (John 16:13). He convinces us that the Bible is God's Word, and the only authority that decides what we should believe and how we should live.

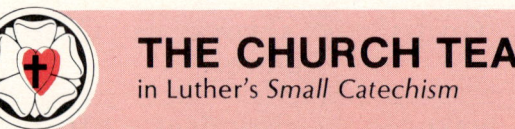

THE CHURCH TEACHES
in Luther's *Small Catechism*

The Work of The Holy Spirit

'I believe that I cannot by my own understanding or effort believe in Jesus Christ my Lord, or come to him. But the Holy Spirit has called me through the Gospel, enlightened me with his gifts, and sanctified and kept me in the true faith.'

OVERVIEW OF THE BIBLE

The 39 Old Testament books were written in Hebrew before the coming of Christ.
The 27 New Testament books were written in Greek after the coming of Christ.

Since Jesus' baptism the dove has been a symbol of the Holy Spirit (see Matthew 3:16). The Spirit uses God's Word to lead us to faith.

NOTES

OLD TESTAMENT

● **History** (Genesis – Esther)
Creation; The Fall into sin; the Flood.
A new beginning: God calls Abraham, and promises to bless the whole world through him and his descendants. The 12 tribes of Israel are God's chosen people. God rescues them from slavery in Egypt, makes his covenant with them, and brings them to Canaan. God rules and blesses them, even though they are unfaithful. Kings are anointed servants of God who rule his people. David is the great king. Later kings are unfaithful to the Lord. The kingdom of Israel is divided. The northern kingdom is destroyed in 721 BC; the southern kingdom ends in 587 BC when the people are taken as exiles to Babylon. Seventy years later, some 40,000 people return and rebuild Jerusalem and the temple.

● **Poetry** (Job – Song of Solomon)
Expressions of the faith of God's people in prayer and praise; Wisdom literature also offers guidelines for godly living.

● **Prophets** (Isaiah – Malachi)
The books of the prophets record the Word of the Lord which the inspired prophets spoke to Israel and/or the nations. They preached the threat of God's judgment, but also the promise of his salvation. Their predictions came true both in their own day, and then also in later times. Prophets foretold the destruction of Jerusalem, but also the return of the exiles from Babylon and the rebuilding of the city and temple. Through the prophets, God gave his promises about the coming Messiah.

NEW TESTAMENT

● **History** (Matthew – Acts)
The four gospels tell the story of Jesus' life, death, and resurrection, and give summaries of Jesus' teaching. Matthew, Mark, and Luke follow the same basic outline.

The Acts of the Apostles is the continuation of Luke's gospel. It describes the coming of the Holy Spirit and the spread of the early Christian church.

● **Epistles** (Romans – Jude)
21 letters by apostles, written to churches and/or individual Christians and read in public worship. The epistles explain the teachings of Jesus and apply them to life.

● **Prophecy**
The book of The Revelation to St John records a vision which describes in picture language the present condition and the future hope of God's church.

MORE TO THINK ABOUT

1 Think about what this chapter is saying to you personally, especially about your attitude toward the Bible, the Bible's teaching about the Triune God, and the messages of the Law and the Gospel. Ask God to send you the Holy Spirit to help you believe his Word.

2 The Bible has sometimes been described as a 'love-letter' from God to us. What do you think of this description?

3 Describe what messages from God you get in the following Bible passages: Isaiah 43:1–13; Luke 8:5–15; Luke 10:38–42.

4 Next time you go to a church service, listen carefully for Law and Gospel messages in the Bible readings and in the sermon.

HE'S GOT THE WHOLE WORLD IN HIS HANDS!

4

OUR WORLD often seems to be in a total mess. So many bad things seem to be piled up against us: war, sickness, accidents, natural disasters, man-made disasters.

We all have our own personal worries and problems, as well.

Is God really 'for us' in our day-to-day life in this troubled world?

JESUS says: **Yes!** God is for us in every part of our daily life.

NOTES

> I tell you, do not worry about your life, what you will eat or drink; or about your body, what you will wear. Is not life more important than food, and the body more important than clothes? Look at the birds of the air; they do not sow or reap or store away in barns, and yet your heavenly Father feeds them. Are you not much more valuable than they? . . .
>
> And why do you worry about clothes? See how the lilies of the field grow. They do not labour or spin. Yet I tell you that not even Solomon in all his splendour was dressed like one of these. If that is how God clothes the grass of the field, which is here today and tomorrow is thrown into the fire, will he not much more clothe you, O you of little faith?
>
> So do not worry, saying, 'What shall we eat?' or 'What shall we drink?' or 'What shall we wear?' For the pagans run after all these things, and your heavenly Father knows that you need them. But seek first his kingdom and his righteousness, and all these things will be given to you as well.
>
> Therefore, do not worry about tomorrow, for tomorrow will worry about itself. Each day has enough trouble of its own.
>
> (Matthew 6:25–34)

GOD IS OUR FATHER

Jesus says that **his** Father is **our** Father. We can be sure that God is **'for us'** in our day-to-day living because:
- He gave us life as his most important creatures
- He loves us and looks after us. He provides, preserves, and protects.

We can trust God as our Father, and can live confidently, yet responsibly, in his world.

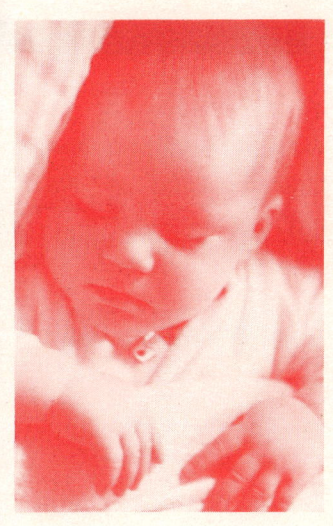

THE ALMIGHTY CREATOR

The God who **'so loved the world that he gave his only Son'** is the Creator of the whole universe.

The Bible says: 'In the beginning God created the heavens and the earth' (Genesis 1:1). Before the beginning of time, only God existed. But God spoke in the beginning; and, by the power of his word, he created the universe out of nothing. By his word he also created all living creatures.

The masterpiece of God's creation was a human being. The Bible says: 'God created man in his own image, in the image of God he created him; male and female he created them' (Genesis 1:27). Adam and Eve were like their Creator: They could think, and decide, and relate to God. They could take care of his creation. They could love.

Everything in our Father's newly-created world was orderly, everything worked in perfect harmony. God saw that his creation was 'very good'.

When we see the beauty and marvellous design of creation, we join in the Bible's songs of praise to God our Creator, and confess: 'I believe that God has created me and all that exists' (Martin Luther).

BIBLE SEARCH

READ **GENESIS 1**, and **2:1–3**

Some of the most important questions human beings ask are:
Who am I?
Where did I come from?
Why am I here?

How does the Bible answer these questions in Genesis 1 and 2?

THE TAKE-OVER BID

At first, Adam and Eve had a perfect life, free of all the evils and worries that bother us. As our Father had intended, they lived in harmony with him, with one another, and with their world.

But that didn't last. The devil (an angel who rebelled) persuaded them that they could be independent of God and control everything for their own purposes.

They disobeyed God. And that ruined everything! The harmony was shattered. All the relationships of human beings were broken: their relationship with God, with themselves, with one another, with creation.

BIBLE SEARCH

READ **GENESIS 3:1–19**

Why did God command Adam and Eve not to eat the fruit from a particular tree?

What causes broken relationships in our world today?

Death came into the world as 'the wages of sin'. And human life became a struggle against death and against everything that threatens us with death.

That's when worry was born! When people declare themselves independent of their Creator/Father, there can only be insecurity and uncertainty about how they will manage.

GOOD NEWS: GOD IS FOR US!

Jesus came to repair the damage caused by the rebellion of human beings against their Maker (called 'the Fall'). He paid the penalty for all sin by his innocent suffering and death.

Jesus came to heal all our broken relationships — with God, with ourselves, with one another, with our world.

Everyone who is led by the Holy Spirit to turn away from sin and to turn to Jesus in faith can now call God 'Father'. If we believe in Jesus as our Saviour, we also believe in God as our Father. And we see him at work as the perfect Father: providing, protecting, preserving his children in a fallen world. He does this even for people who still reject him. The Bible says: 'He makes his sun to rise on the evil and the good, and sends rain on the righteous and the unrighteous' (Matthew 5:45).

Our Father has not washed his hands of us; he does not leave us to battle alone against all those things which seem to be piled up against us.

Our Father

- **provides** Through nature, through people, through our daily work, he gives us our bodily needs.

- **preserves** He keeps the world, its beauty, and all its resources, for the sake of his children. He controls the course of history.

- **protects** His angels have the special responsibility of keeping his children from all harm and danger.

NOTES

BIBLE SEARCH

READ **PSALM 145:15,16**

If God supplies food for all, why do some people go hungry?

Have there been striking examples of God's care and protection in your life?

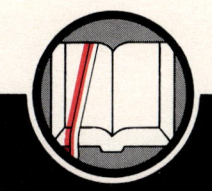

KEY BIBLE STATEMENTS

- In the beginning God created the heavens and the earth. (Genesis 1:1)

- By him [Jesus] all things were created: things in heaven and on earth, visible and invisible... all things were created by him and for him. He is before all things, and in him all things hold together. (Colossians 1:16,17)

- I praise you because I am fearfully and wonderfully made; your works are wonderful, I know that full well. (Psalm 139:14)

- Cast all your anxiety on him because he cares for you. (1 Peter 5:7)

- He will command his angels concerning you to guard you in all your ways. (Psalm 91:11)

- Give thanks to the Lord for he is good; his love endures for ever. (Psalm 118:1)

WHY DO THINGS GO WRONG?

We still have to live with many consequences of sin: wars, famines, disasters, personal problems. Yet in all these things God is still **for us.** Believing in God as our Father means trusting his promise: **'In all things God works for the good of those who love him'** (Romans 8:28).

We don't always know exactly why God allows suffering; he doesn't always explain his purposes to us. But he does give us his promise to hold on to: **'[Nothing] in all creation will be able to separate us from the love of God that is in Christ Jesus our Lord'** (Romans 8:39).

Our Father knows. Our Father cares. Our Father is in control. We can trust him all the way. (Read again Matthew 6:25-34.)

RESPONSIBLE CHILDREN

When we believe our Father is for us, we can live confidently. But we will also live responsibly in his world. We will acknowledge our place — not as absolute owners, but as responsible caretakers. As we enjoy the gift of his wonderful creation, as we experience his loving care, we will praise our Father/Creator. And we will use his gifts to do his will in the world — because he is our Father.

THE CHURCH TEACHES
in Luther's *Small Catechism*

(from the Apostles' Creed)

The First Article
I believe in God the Father almighty, Maker of heaven and earth.
What does this mean?
I believe that God has created me and all that exists. He has given me and still preserves my body and soul with all their powers. He provides me with food and clothing, home and family, daily work, and all I need from day to day. God also protects me in time of danger and guards me from every evil. All this he does out of fatherly and divine goodness and mercy, though I do not deserve it. Therefore I surely ought to thank and praise, serve and obey him.
This is most certainly true.

MORE TO THINK ABOUT

1 Think about what this chapter is saying to you personally about God and yourself. Does this chapter call for any changes in your ...beliefs? ...attitudes? ...conduct? ...lifestyle?

2 We are able to enjoy and use God's wonderful creation. But what responsibility do we have over against creation? How does believing in our Father as the almighty Creator affect our attitude toward creation? How does God involve us in his work of providing, preserving, and protecting?

3 In itself, sex is a good gift of our Creator. It is meant for our happiness. How does human selfishness or self-centredness spoil God's good gift?

4 Check the following Bible readings: Psalm 8 — Our great Creator; Genesis 3 — The Fall; Genesis 6,7,8 — God saves Noah; Psalm 23 — The Lord is my shepherd; Matthew 14:13-21 — Jesus provides food.

BAPTISM: GOD IS FOR ME! **5**

'GOD SO LOVED the world...' 'Jesus died for all.' The Bible is full of statements like that, emphasizing that God is for all people.

That's great! But it's not very personal. 'The world' means billions of people — but I need to be sure that God is for **me**. The good news of God's love for everybody needs to become personal.

Baptism is one way in which God comes to each one of us personally with his love. When I am baptized, I can be sure: God is **for me**!

NOTE:

Lutherans use the word 'sacrament' to describe holy acts which

- are commanded by God
- use God's Word with earthly elements
- offer and give the forgiveness Jesus won for us.

According to this definition, there are two sacraments: Baptism and the Lord's Supper.

'I BAPTIZE YOU...'

AFTER HIS DEATH and resurrection, Jesus commanded his followers: 'Go and make disciples of all nations, baptizing them in the name of the Father and of the Son and of the Holy Spirit' (Matthew 28:19). He thereby 'instituted' or established the Sacrament of Holy Baptism.

Baptism is a very simple act. To 'baptize' means to apply water to a person. The water used in Baptism is ordinary water, and it makes no difference how the water is applied — whether by sprinkling, washing, pouring, or immersing. Jesus gave no directions about this.

All people need to be baptized. In our 'natural' condition (the way all people are at birth) we're a mess! No baby is born innocent or perfect; it has the sin and guilt of the human race, passed on through its parents. As a child grows, this 'inherited' sin soon shows itself; the child will naturally do what is wrong rather than what is right.

The Bible describes the natural state in which we were born as being

- **spiritually dead** ('You were dead in your transgressions and sins', Ephesians 2:1)
- **spiritually blind** ('The man without the Spirit does not accept the things that come from the Spirit of God, for they are foolishness to him, and he cannot understand them', 1 Corinthians 2:14)
- **enemies of God** ('The sinful mind is hostile to God', Romans 8:7)

What a mess! If God didn't wash us clean and make us new persons, we would still be in this natural condition.

WASHED CLEAN

Because God is for us, he sent Jesus to rescue us from our natural sinful condition. Jesus paid for all our sins. Then he instituted Baptism as God's way of handing over to each one of us personally all the blessings Jesus won for the whole world.

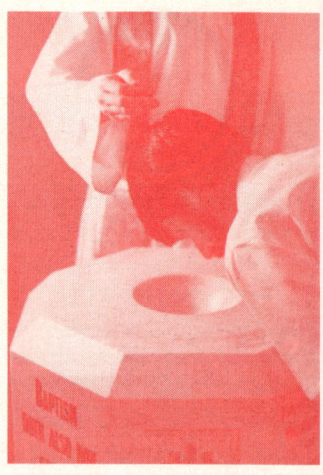

NOTES

BIBLE SEARCH

READ **JOHN 3:1–6**

How would you have felt if you were Nicodemus, and Jesus said to you: 'You must be born again'?

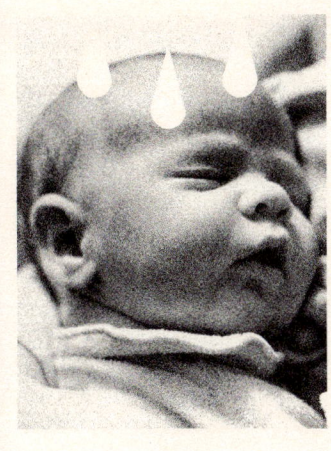

So, through Baptism
- God **forgives** all our sins
- God **sets us free** from the power of death and the devil
- God **gives** us everlasting life.

In Baptism, God washes us clean from all the guilt we were born with, and from all the sins we have committed or will commit. Through Baptism, God makes us new people. We are born again as his children to live a new life. We become members of his family.

'IN THE NAME OF . . .'

The mere applying of water can't do all this for us. Water can't wash away sins. What gives Baptism its special power is the fact that **God's Word** is used with the water according to Jesus' command: **'Baptiz[e all nations] in the name of the Father and of the Son and of the Holy Spirit'** (Matthew 28:19).

The 'name' of God means everything God is as Father, Son, and Holy Spirit. The power of the Triune God is at work in Baptism:

The Father who created and loves the world, becomes **your** Father. He adopts you as his child.

The Son who saved the whole world, becomes **your** Saviour. In Baptism, you are connected to Christ's death and resurrection. You, with all your sin, die with him. You rise again with him to a new and holy life.

The Holy Spirit who is 'the Lord and giver of life', gives **you** new life as a child of God and a member of God's family. The power of the Holy Spirit works in you, so that you believe in Jesus, and accept his forgiveness, life, and salvation.

A PERSONAL PACT

'I baptize you in the name of the Father and of the Son and of the Holy Spirit.' This is God's way of claiming you, of putting his brand on you and saying: 'You belong to me from now on. You're in my family.'

A symbol of Baptism. Through water and the Word, the Triune God (three rings interlocked) gives us new life as his children.

BIBLE SEARCH

READ **TITUS 3:3–7**

What great things does God do through Baptism? (See also Galatians 3:26–28.)

NOTES

An ancient symbol of Baptism. The three drops of water represent the Father, Son, and Holy Spirit.

God puts his name to a personal covenant (pact or agreement) he makes with you: 'I am your Father, you are my child. I will always love you and bless you.'

It is God who takes the initiative and does all the giving in Baptism. He offers his grace, forgiveness, and eternal life to everyone who is baptized. We accept these gifts by faith, by trusting the Word God speaks to us in Baptism.

Faith is important. Jesus said: '**Whoever believes and is baptized will be saved, but whoever does not believe will be condemned**' (Mark 16:16). By faith we draw on the benefits of Baptism again and again throughout our life.

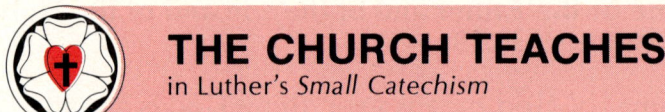

THE CHURCH TEACHES
in Luther's *Small Catechism*

The Sacrament of Holy Baptism

1. What is Baptism?
Baptism is not water only, but it is water used together with God's Word and by his command.

What is this Word?
In Matthew 28 our Lord Jesus Christ says:
'Go therefore and make disciples of all nations, baptizing them in the name of the Father and of the Son and of the Holy Spirit.'

2. What benefits does God give in Baptism?
In Baptism God forgives sin, delivers from death and the devil, and gives everlasting salvation to all who believe what he has promised.

What is God's promise?
In Mark 16 our Lord Jesus Christ says:
'He who believes and is baptized will be saved; but he who does not believe will be condemned.'

3. How can water do such great things?
It is not water that does these things, but God's Word with the water and our trust in this Word. Water by itself is only water, but with the Word of God it is a life-giving water which by grace gives the new birth through the Holy Spirit.

St Paul writes in Titus 3:
'He saved us... in virtue of his own mercy, by the washing of regeneration and renewal in the Holy Spirit, which he poured out upon us richly through Jesus Christ our Saviour, so that we might be justified by his grace and become heirs in hope of eternal life. The saying is sure.'

NOTES

KEY BIBLE STATEMENTS

● Unless a man is born of water and the Spirit, he cannot enter the kingdom of God. Flesh gives birth to flesh, but the Spirit gives birth to spirit. (John 3:5,6)

● Repent and be baptized, every one of you, in the name of Jesus Christ so that your sins may be forgiven. And you will receive the gift of the Holy Spirit. (Acts 2:38)

● Be baptized and wash your sins away, calling on his name. (Acts 22:16)

● [Jesus said:] Let the little children come to me, and do not hinder them, for the kingdom of God belongs to such as these. I tell you the truth, anyone who will not receive the kingdom of God like a little child will never enter it. (Mark 10:14)

4 What does Baptism mean for daily living?
It means that our sinful self, with all its evil deeds and desires, should be drowned through daily repentance; and that day after day a new self should arise to live with God in righteousness and purity for ever.

St Paul writes in Romans 6:
'We were buried therefore with him by baptism into death, so that as Christ was raised from the dead by the glory of the Father, we too might walk in newness of life.'

BAPTISM IS FOR ALL

Baptism is for everyone, young and old. Jesus did not set any age-limit. He simply commanded us to baptize *'all nations'*.

Some Christians believe that only those people should be baptized who are old enough to make a conscious decision for God. But it is God who does the deciding in Baptism. He wants to make *his* personal covenant with all people — even with new-born babies, because they, too, need to be washed and to be born again.

That is why we baptize infants. The Holy Spirit creates the miracle of faith even in infants through Baptism. As the children grow up, we teach them what it means to be baptized in the name of the Father, Son, and Holy Spirit, so that they can appreciate the blessings of Baptism. This teaching needs to go on throughout their lives, so that they never lose the benefits or blessings of Baptism, but draw on them all their lives.

Baptism gives us power for Christian living (see chapter six). When Martin Luther felt depressed, or was being bothered by sin and temptation, he would sometimes cry out: 'But I am baptized!'

Baptism is my lifelong guarantee that God is **for me**!

MORE TO THINK ABOUT

1 Think about what this chapter is saying to you personally about God and yourself. Does this chapter call for any changes in your ...beliefs? ...attitudes? ...conduct? ...lifestyle?

2 Read the following Bible stories of how Jesus' followers began to carry out his command to make disciples by baptizing and teaching: Acts 2:1–42; Acts 8:26–40; Acts 16:16–34.

3 'It is in infant baptism that the Gospel is proclaimed loudest in the church; for here it is quite clear that in God's sight man is a being who **receives** ... A child shows what real faith means: to be in God's presence with empty hands, to be dependent on him. God gives his promises even without man's understanding.' (From *One in the Gospel* by Friedemann Hebart, Lutheran Publishing House, 1979).

4 Can a person go to heaven if he/she is not baptized? (Luke 23:39–43 might help.)

5 Why do we begin our church services 'in the name of the Father and of the Son and of the Holy Spirit'?

POWER FOR LIVING   6

DO YOU NOTICE any difference at all between people who are Christians and people who are not?

In what ways would you expect becoming a Christian to make a big difference in a person's life? Should life become easier or harder? Would there be fewer problems or more?

IF WE HAVE been baptized, we are 'born-again Christians'. Through Baptism, God gives new life; he makes new people. That means a new and different lifestyle.

What's different about the way Christians live?

In the first place, our relationship with God is different. We don't ignore God, or run away from him, or try to keep him out of our lives. We believe in him, and trust him in every part of life.

When we know God as our loving Father who has accepted us, forgiven and adopted us in amazing grace, we no longer feel that it's up to us to make a good impression on him, or to try to get into his good books and win his approval. We believe he is already **for us**.

WE'RE FREE!

That means that we are free from certain things:

- We have been set free from the demands and accusations of God's Law
- We have been set free from the guilt and power of sin
- We have been set free from the punishment of sin. (We may still have to live with the *consequences* of sin. But nothing that happens in the life of Christians is ever a punishment from God.)

We who believe that God is for us should no longer live as slaves under God's Law, or as slaves to sin. We should live as people who have been set free to serve God. The Bible says: **'You have been set free from sin and have become slaves to righteousness'** (Romans 6:18).

UNDER NEW MANAGEMENT

As God's children through Baptism and through faith in Jesus, we are 'under new management'. The Holy Spirit, who brought us to faith, is the new manager. He comes

NOTES

BIBLE SEARCH

READ **COLOSSIANS 3:1–17**

What changes does God want to see in our lives according to verses 2, 12, and 17?

to live in us. His power is at work in us, 'sanctifying' us, making us holy. He helps us to live as God's children — as children who are a credit to their Father. We begin to lead holy lives, to do things that are good in the sight of God — not to get God on our side, but *because* he already *is* on our side.

Christian faith shows itself in Christian living. That's the great work of the Holy Spirit: He produces faith that is active in love. The Bible says: **'The fruit of the Spirit is love, joy, peace, patience, kindness, goodness, faithfulness, gentleness and self-control'**

(Galatians 5:22,23).

SAINTS AND SINNERS

But that is only one side of the picture of how Christians live. The truth is that we don't always let the Spirit control us. We don't always behave as children of our Father in heaven. We don't always make good, right, God-pleasing decisions. Sometimes we don't even bother to ask what is our Father's will. Sometimes we may even begin to wonder whether we really are God's children, under new management.

If we are Christians, why do we so often find it hard to live a good life? Why do we live under the tension of knowing what is right but also wanting to do what is wrong? We almost seem to be two different people.

We *do* have two different natures — that's the trouble! We still have our old sinful nature in us. The sinful self was drowned in Baptism, but it won't lie down; it keeps on trying to take over again. So, as long as we live on earth, we are both saints and sinners at the same time. Our life as Christians is a struggle between the old and new natures.

THE HOLY SPIRIT OUR HELPER

We need help in the struggle to live a Christian life. We need the power of the Holy Spirit working in us. The Spirit's power is at work in us whenever we hear or read God's Word, and whenever we receive the sacrament of Holy Communion. God's Word and the Sacraments are 'means of grace'.

THE MEANS OF GRACE
God's Word, Baptism, and Holy Communion are called 'the means of grace', because they are the ways God uses to bring his love to us.

NOTES

BIBLE SEARCH

READ **Romans 7:14–25**

Is there any way in which you identify with St Paul here and say: 'Yes, I know from my own experience what he's talking about'?

Through Baptism the Holy Spirit not only gives us new life, but also gives us power to live as God's children.

THE HOLY SPIRIT — GOD FOR US

- The Holy Spirit uses God's **Law** to show us our sins and our need for God's forgiveness. Through the Law he keeps us from trusting in our own goodness or good deeds.

- The Holy Spirit uses the **Gospel** to make us sure of God's forgiveness in Jesus day by day, so that we don't despair when we seem to be losing the battle against our sinful self.

- The Holy Spirit brings us close to Jesus. When in faith we hear or read God's Word, when we remember our baptism, when we receive Holy Communion, the Spirit makes our faith in Jesus stronger. That faith becomes a more powerful force in our lives, controlling our thoughts and actions more and more.

It is not easy to live the life of a child of God. We have many ups and downs. Every day we have to face temptations and tests — not only from our own sinful nature, but also from Satan, and from people whom Satan uses to put pressure on us.

The Christian life follows a cycle of sin and forgiveness. We never reach the stage here on earth of being perfect. But the good news is that the Holy Spirit is 'God for us'. He keeps on offering us God's grace, and he gives us the faith to trust only in that grace.

With the Spirit at work in us, we can live victoriously as God's children.

BIBLE SEARCH

WHAT DO the following Bible passages tell us about the Holy Spirit and his work?

John 15:26; John 16:12–15; Romans 8:9–17; 1 Corinthians 12:4–11.

NOTES

KEY BIBLE STATEMENTS

- We love because he first loved us.
  (1 John 4:19)

- No one can say, 'Jesus is Lord', except by the Holy Spirit.
  (1 Corinthians 12:3)

- Create in me a pure heart, O God, and renew a steadfast spirit within me. Do not cast me from your presence or take your Holy Spirit from me.
  (Psalm 51:10,11)

- He [Christ] died for all, that those who live should no longer live for themselves but for him who died for them and was raised again ... If anyone is in Christ, he is a new creation.
  (2 Corinthians 5:15,17)

- [Jesus said:] I am the vine; you are the branches. If a man remains in me and I in him, he will bear much fruit; apart from me you can do nothing.
  (John 15:5)

- He who began a good work in you will carry it on to completion until the day of Christ Jesus.
  (Philippians 1:6)

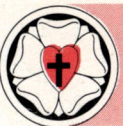

THE CHURCH TEACHES
in Luther's *Small Catechism*

(from The Apostles' Creed)

The Third Article
I believe in the Holy Spirit; the holy Christian church, the communion of saints; the forgiveness of sins; the resurrection of the body; and the life everlasting. Amen.
What does this mean?
I believe that I cannot by my own understanding or effort believe in Jesus Christ, my Lord, or come to him. But the Holy Spirit has called me through the Gospel, enlightened me with his gifts, and sanctified and kept me in true faith.
In the same way he calls, gathers, enlightens, and sanctifies the whole Christian church on earth, and keeps it united with Jesus Christ in the one true faith.
In this Christian church day after day he fully forgives my sins and the sins of all believers. On the last day he will raise me and all the dead, and give me and all believers in Christ eternal life.
This is most certainly true.

(from Baptism)

What does Baptism mean for daily living?
   It means that our sinful self, with all its evil deeds and desires, should be drowned through daily repentance; and that day after day a new self should arise to live with God in righteousness and purity for ever.
St Paul writes in Romans 6:
'We were buried therefore with him by baptism into death, so that as Christ was raised from the dead by the glory of the Father, we too might walk in newness of life.'

MORE TO THINK ABOUT

1 Think about what this chapter is saying to you personally about God and yourself, especially about your way of life. Does it call for any changes in your ... beliefs? ... attitudes? ... conduct? ... lifestyle?

2 Read the following Bible passages, and note what they say about various aspects of Christian living:
1 Corinthians 13 — about love
Galatians 5:16–25 — about the work of the Holy Spirit
John 15:1–17 — about being joined to Jesus
Mark 8:34–38 — about following Jesus.

3 Read Matthew chapters 5, 6, and 7 (the Sermon on the Mount). List some of the ways in which Christians are to be different from other people.

4 Think of special problems or sins you wrestle with in your own life. Where can you find help in your struggle? (Ephesians 6:10–18 may help.)

GOD FOR US — FOR SURE!

7

WHY DO WE sometimes think it important to check out the guarantee on something we want to buy? Why are guarantees necessary?

What guarantee does God give us that he is really for us?

WHEN WE BELIEVE in Jesus as our Saviour, we are God's children. The Gospel tells us that quite clearly. And that is the message of our baptism, too.

But sometimes we are not sure about this. Many Christians experience doubts about whether God really does love them — especially when they don't seem to be able to break away from sinning against him. We too may find it hard to live in the confidence that nothing will separate us from the Father's love.

Does God really forgive us for everything and anything, completely and for ever? We need reassurance — some kind of guarantee.

Holy Communion is God's guarantee of his love. Through this sacrament, God says to us again and again: 'I am for you — for sure! You need never doubt my grace and forgiveness.'

Holy Communion is also a special way in which we celebrate everything Jesus has done for us, and give thanks to God for his amazing grace.

Guaranteed for a LIFETIME!!

N O T E S

THE LORD'S SUPPER

On the evening before he died, Jesus ate the Passover meal with his disciples. In the Passover festival, the Jews remembered how God had saved their ancestors from slavery in Egypt. When the angel of death went through the land, he 'passed over' those homes of the Israelites which had the blood of a lamb smeared on the doorposts. So, in the Passover a lamb was killed and eaten as a celebration of God's saving act.

After celebrating the Passover, Jesus gave a new meal to his followers. They had something new to celebrate: Jesus' death as the Lamb of God who gave his life to save all people. This meal celebrated the new covenant in which God offers his love and forgiveness to people of every nation.

The Bible describes how Jesus instituted his Supper:

Our Lord Jesus Christ on the night when he was betrayed took bread, and when he had given thanks, he broke it and gave it to his disciples and said, 'Take and eat; this is my body, which is given for you. Do this in remembrance of me.'

In the same way he took the cup after the supper, and when he had given thanks, he gave it to them and said, 'Drink of it all of you; this is my blood of the new covenant, which is shed for you for the forgiveness of sins. Do this, as often as you drink it, in remembrance of me.'

(Words of Institution, based on Matthew 26:26–28; Mark 14:22–24; Luke 22:19,20; and 1 Corinthians 11:23–25.)

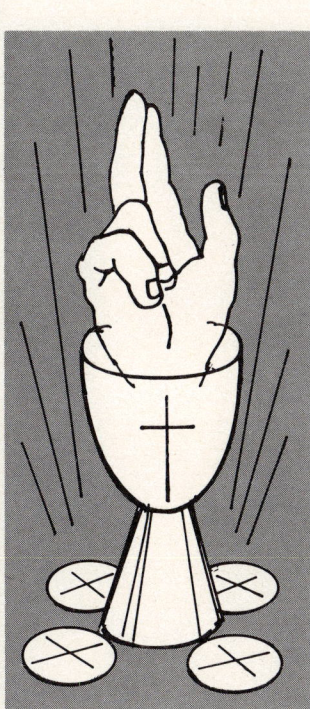

THE REAL PRESENCE

Whenever we celebrate Holy Communion, these events described in the Bible are brought into our time. Jesus is present as the Host who sets his meal before us. He gives us bread to eat and wine to drink. As he gives us the bread, he says: 'This is my body, which is given **for you**.' As he gives us the wine, he says: 'This is my blood of the new covenant, which is shed **for you** for the forgiveness of sins.'

We eat the bread and drink the wine in a normal, natural way. But at the same time, in a way we can't explain or understand, we also eat and drink the true body and blood of our living Lord — the same body and blood which he offered on the cross as the perfect sacrifice for our sins.

'This **is** my body . . . This **is** my blood', Jesus says. This is not just a picture or symbol that we have here; our Lord's body and blood are truly present with the bread and wine. We believe his Word.

GOD'S GUARANTEE

Why does Jesus give us his body and blood in this sacrament? Because that is the price he paid to set us free from sin, death, and the power of the devil. With his body and blood which were 'given and shed' for us, our

NOTES

BIBLE SEARCH

READ
1 CORINTHIANS 11:23–26

In the Lord's Supper Jesus gives us

...*something to eat and drink* — his body and blood with bread and wine

...*something to remember* — that he gave his body and shed his blood **for us**

...*something to proclaim* — that he died and rose again as the Saviour of the world

...*something to look forward to* — the never-ending feast with him in heaven. Holy Communion is a 'preview' of heaven.

Lord gives us all the blessings he has won for us: forgiveness, peace, everlasting life. Holy Communion is God's special way of saying: 'You can be sure that I am for you'.

Jesus offers his blessings to all who commune. All who take Communion receive the body and blood of Jesus, whether they believe this or not. But only those who believe in Jesus — that he gave his body and shed his blood for them — get the benefits he offers.

- The Lord's Supper is for **sinners**. No one should ever think: 'I am not good enough to go to Communion'. Jesus' invitation is especially for people who are 'hungry and thirsty' for God's forgiveness.

- The Lord's Supper is for **believers**, and for believers only. Jesus invites all who are sorry for their sins and who believe that he gave his body and shed his blood for them. This sacrament is especially for believers whose faith is weak. The Holy Spirit uses this 'means of grace' to build up our faith, to make us sure that God has forgiven us.

You are Invited

- The Lord's Supper is for **the family of believers**. It is a 'communion' — a fellowship with our Lord and with one another. It is a family celebration in which we say: 'We all believe Jesus died for us. We celebrate his death and his living presence with us. We are one body. We are one in our faith. We believe and confess the same things about Christ and his Supper.'

GETTING READY

The Lord's Supper is a joyful celebration, because in it our Lord gives us such precious gifts. At the same time, we treat the sacrament seriously — just because it is so special. The Bible itself warns: **'Whoever eats the bread or drinks the cup of the Lord in an unworthy manner will be guilty of sinning against the body and blood of the Lord. [Everyone] ought to examine himself before he eats of the bread and drinks of the cup'**
(1 Corinthians 11:27,28).

So, before we go to Communion we should ask ourselves:

1 Am I truly sorry for my sins?

2 Do I truly believe that Jesus died for me, and do I believe that he gives me his body and blood in the sacrament as a guarantee of forgiveness?

3 Do I honestly intend, with God's help, to fight against sin and to live as God's child?

If we can sincerely answer Yes to those questions, we are ready to receive the Lord's Supper.

However, we have to be careful that we don't make this preparation for Communion a 'performance' we put on to 'qualify' for the sacrament. We are not meant to focus on what *we do*, but on what *God has done* and *still does* for us. Luther says: 'That person is well prepared and worthy who believes these words: *given and shed for you for the forgiveness of sins* … The words *for you* require simply a believing heart.'

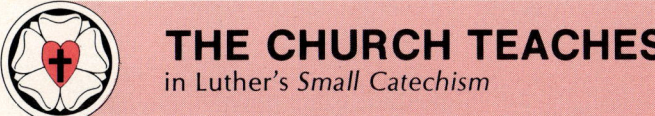

THE CHURCH TEACHES
in Luther's *Small Catechism*

The Sacrament of Holy Communion

 What is Holy Communion?
Holy Communion is the true body and blood of our Lord Jesus Christ given with bread and wine, instituted by Christ himself for us to eat and drink.

Where do the Scriptures say this?
Matthew, Mark, Luke, and Paul say:
Our Lord Jesus Christ on the night when he was betrayed, took bread; and when he had given thanks, he broke it and gave it to his disciples, and said, 'Take and eat; this is my body, which is given for you; do this in remembrance of me.'
In the same way he took the cup, after the supper, and when he had given thanks, he gave it to them, and said 'Drink of it, all of you; this is my blood of the new covenant which is shed for you for the forgiveness of sins; do this, as often as you drink it, in remembrance of me.'

BIBLE SEARCH

READ
1 CORINTHIANS 11:27–29

Why should we examine ourselves before we go to the Lord's Supper?

NOTES

KEY BIBLE STATEMENTS

- [Jesus said:] Come to me, all you who are weary and burdened, and I will give you rest. (Matthew 11:28)

- [Jesus said:] Whoever comes to me I will never drive away. (John 6:37)

- [Jesus said:] I am the bread of life. He who comes to me will never go hungry, and he who believes in me will never be thirsty. (John 6:35)

- Is not the cup of thanksgiving for which we give thanks a participation in the blood of Christ? And is not the bread that we break a participation in the body of Christ? (1 Corinthians 10:16)

- Whenever you eat this bread and drink this cup, you proclaim the Lord's death until he comes. (1 Corinthians 11:26)

2 What benefits do we receive from this sacrament?
The benefits of this sacrament are pointed out by the words: *given and shed for you for the forgiveness of sins*. These words assure us that in the sacrament we receive forgiveness of sins, life, and salvation. For where there is forgiveness of sins, there is also life and salvation.

3 How can eating and drinking do all this?
It is not eating and drinking that does this, but the words: *given and shed for you for the forgiveness of sins*. These words, along with eating and drinking, are the main thing in the sacrament. And whoever believes these words has exactly what they say: forgiveness of sins.

4 When is a person rightly prepared to receive this sacrament?
Fasting and other outward preparations serve a good purpose. However, that person is well prepared and worthy who believes these words: *given and shed for you for the forgiveness of sins*. But anyone who does not believe these words, or doubts them, is neither prepared nor worthy, for the words *for you* require simply a believing heart.

MORE TO THINK ABOUT

1 Think about what this chapter is saying to you personally about God and yourself, especially about God's invitation to his Supper. Does this chapter call for any changes in your ... beliefs? ... attitudes? ... conduct? ... lifestyle?

2 Read John 6, where Jesus calls himself 'the Bread of Life'.

3 How do you react to the following:
a) 'It's no good me going to Communion. No matter how hard I try, I keep on doing the same old sins. I'll only bring God's judgment on myself.'
b) 'I don't feel any different after I've been to Communion. Can we be sure that we are forgiven if we don't *feel* forgiven?'
c) 'Communion is really a great idea. I can do what I like during the week, then on Sunday I can go to Communion and square things up with God again.'

4 How often should we receive Communion?

WE ARE THE CHURCH

8

THE WORD 'church' can have several meanings. Pinpoint what is meant by 'church' in the following:

'There's a new church down the road.'

'What time's church?'

'Our church is getting a new minister.'

'The church ought to do more for poor people.'

THE HOLY CHRISTIAN CHURCH

'**I WILL BUILD** my church', Jesus promised his disciples (Matthew 16:19). He was not talking about a place where people meet for worship. Nor did he mean the man-made organizations we call 'church' — the different denominations, which have as members both sincere believers and people who are Christians only by name.

The Church of Jesus Christ is the community of all people who believe in him as their Lord. It is God's family. All its members are 'saints' — people whom God regards as holy because they have had their sins forgiven. So, it is called the **holy** Christian Church.

We don't join this Church by our own decision; the Holy Spirit makes us members by calling us through the Gospel, leading us to faith in Jesus, and gathering us into God's family.

GOD'S HOLY PEOPLE

The word 'church' in the Bible means people who have been 'called out' by God. In the Old Testament, God called out the nation of Israel to be his own special people. They were a 'holy' nation — a nation 'set apart' for his special purposes, to bring blessing to all peoples.

When Jesus came, he called 12 disciples as the first members of the new people of God: Jesus' Church. 'You are the blessed ones', he told his disciples. 'You are the salt of the earth and the light of the world' (Matthew 6:13–16). After his resurrection, Jesus sent the Holy Spirit at Pentecost to call and gather people from many nations through the Gospel into the one holy Christian Church.

The Holy Spirit is the builder of the Christian Church. His 'building tools' are God's Word and the Sacraments. He uses the preaching and witnessing of God's people to lead others into the Church.

NOTES

BIBLE SEARCH

The Bible uses pictures to describe Jesus' church.

READ **1 Corinthians 12:12–27**

The Church is the BODY OF CHRIST.

Why is Jesus called the Head?

Who are the members of the Body?

What is the relationship of each member to the Head and to other members?

How does this picture show that membership in Christ's Church is a 'full-time' occupation?

The one holy Christian Church is 'catholic' or universal. It exists all over the world, wherever the Spirit is at work through God's Word and Sacraments. We can't tell who the members of this Church are, but **'the Lord knows those who are his'** (2 Timothy 2:19).

ONE CHURCH — MANY DENOMINATIONS

There is only **one** holy Christian Church, but there are many different denominations (e.g., Lutheran, Roman Catholic, Baptist, etc.). Denominations arise because people understand and explain the Bible differently. No one denomination can rightly claim to be the one holy Christian Church, for the Church is made up of all people who believe in Jesus. There are members of Christ's Church in every Christian denomination wherever the Holy Spirit is at work through the Gospel.

We rightly work and pray for unity between the denominations. But the Spirit has already created a bond of unity between all believers in Christ, no matter what denomination they belong to. The Bible says: 'There is one body and one Spirit . . . one Lord, one faith, one baptism; one God and Father of all . . .' (Ephesians 4:4–6).

THE CHURCH IN ACTION

The Holy Spirit calls us to be God's Church in our own community. So we form *congregations* — gatherings of Christians in a certain locality.

The most important work of a congregation is to use the means of grace: to preach and teach God's Word, to administer Baptism, to celebrate Holy Communion. Every member of the congregation has the responsibility of supporting this work.

A SPECIAL POWER

Jesus has given every Christian and every congregation the authority to open or close the 'door' of heaven in his name. The door of heaven is opened to those who repent of their sins and believe in Jesus when we tell them: 'Your sins are forgiven'. The door of heaven is closed to those who don't repent or believe when we tell them: 'Your sins are not forgiven'. This is called **'the power of the keys'**. We use the power of the keys whenever we use God's Word and Sacraments.

God's Word and Sacraments are the keys that open and close the 'doors' of heaven.

BIBLE SEARCH

READ **Ephesians 2:19–22**
The Church is the TEMPLE OF GOD.

Why is Jesus called the 'cornerstone' of his Church?

Why are the apostles and prophets called the 'foundation' of the Church?

What does it mean to be a 'living stone' in the temple of God?

NOTES

God has given his Church the authority to lock and unlock heaven through preaching his Word and using the Sacraments.

THE OFFICE OF THE MINISTRY

Christ's gifts to his Church include pastors or ministers (Ephesians 4:11). Every congregation has the right to call a pastor to carry out the public preaching and teaching of God's Word, and to administer the Sacraments on behalf of the congregation.

A pastor also has the responsibility to equip members of the congregation for their ministry as the people of God. The Bible says that every Christian is a 'priest'. This means:

● Every Christian is set apart to serve God in his or her calling in life

● Every Christian has the power of the keys

● Every Christian can go directly to the Father in Jesus' name

● Every Christian bears witness to Jesus by words and actions.

CHURCH MEMBERSHIP

We need our fellow-Christians. We need the Church family. But how can we tell which church to belong to? Here are some guidelines:

● What matters first and foremost is that we are members of the one holy Christian Church by being baptized and believing in Jesus through the power of the Holy Spirit.

● We need to be satisfied that the denomination we belong to, or are thinking of joining, teaches what the Bible says and uses the Sacraments in the way God has commanded. We need to avoid any church or organization which teaches falsely about Christ and his Word.

● We should be active members of our local congregation, attending worship regularly, helping in the ministry of caring, using the gifts God has given us to serve him and other people, and gladly offering our financial support.

BIBLE SEARCH

READ 1 PETER 2:9,10

What titles are used to describe Christians?

For what purpose has God made us his own people?

How can you act as a 'priest' of God?

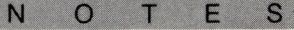

N O T E S

KEY BIBLE STATEMENTS

- [Jesus said:] My sheep listen to my voice; I know them, and they follow me. I give them eternal life, and they shall never perish; no one can snatch them out of my hand. (John 10:27,28)

- In Christ we who are many form one body, and each member belongs to all the others. (Romans 12:5)

- [Jesus said:] If you hold to my teaching, you are really my disciples. Then you will know the truth, and the truth will set you free. (John 8:31,32)

- They [the first Christians] devoted themselves to the apostles' teaching and to the fellowship, to the breaking of bread and to prayer. (Acts 2:42)

- You are a chosen people, a royal priesthood, a holy nation, a people belonging to God, that you may declare the praises of him who called you out of darkness into his wonderful light. (1 Peter 2:9)

THE CHURCH TEACHES
in Luther's *Small Catechism*

(from The Apostles' Creed)

THE THIRD ARTICLE

I believe in the Holy Spirit; the holy Christian Church, the communion of saints; the forgiveness of sins; the resurrection of the body; and the life everlasting. Amen.

What does this mean?

I believe that I cannot by my own understanding or effort believe in Jesus Christ, my Lord, or come to him. But the Holy Spirit has called me through the Gospel, enlightened me with his gifts, and sanctified and kept me in true faith. In the same way he calls, gathers, enlightens, and sanctifies the whole Christian Church on earth and keeps it united with Jesus Christ in the one true faith. In this Christian Church day after day he fully forgives my sins and the sins of all believers. On the last day he will raise me and all the dead and give me and all believers in Christ eternal life. This is most certainly true.

(from The Office of the Keys*)

What is the 'Office of the Keys'?

It is that authority which Christ gave to his Church to forgive the sins of those who repent and to declare to those who do not repent that their sins are not forgiven.

What are the words of Christ?

Our Lord Jesus Christ said to his disciples: 'Receive the Holy Spirit. If you forgive the sins of any, they are forgiven; if you retain the sins of any, they are retained' (John 20:23).

'Truly, I say to you, Whatever you bind on earth shall be bound in heaven, and whatever you loose on earth shall be loosed in heaven' (Matthew 18:18).

*The Office of the Keys was not written by Luther, but was later taken up into the *Small Catechism*.

MORE TO THINK ABOUT

1 Think about what this chapter is saying to you personally about the Church. Does this chapter call for any significant changes in your ... beliefs? ... attitudes? ... conduct? ... lifestyle?

2 In Acts 2, read the story of how the Holy Spirit brought 3000 people into the Church in one day.

3 Read 1 Corinthians 12:12–27. What does this passage say about what we can expect from other Christians, and what other Christians can expect from us?

4 What might new members in a congregation be able to do in a better way than old members?

5 'Christians are not perfect — just forgiven.' What does this say to us about the Church.

FULL-TIME CHRISTIANITY　9

MANY ASPECTS of life involve commitment. What kind of commitment is required, for example:

...to get to the top in a career?

...to become a 'star' in sport, music, etc.?

...in marriage and family relationships?

WHAT DOES it cost to be a Christian? There are two ways of answering this question:

- It costs *nothing* to *become* a Christian! God has done everything for us. He gives us everything free of charge simply because he is totally **for us** (cf Ephesians 2:8).

- It costs *everything* to *be* a Christian! When the Holy Spirit leads us to believe in Jesus, we belong to him completely. Our Lord asks for total commitment when he commands us: 'Follow me!' Following Jesus costs us our life (cf Luke 14:33).

It's impossible to be a 'part-time' Christian, a part-time 'arm' or 'leg' in the Body of Christ. The call to follow Jesus is a call to full-time Christianity.

FULL-TIME WORSHIP

Full-time Christianity means a life of worship. The word 'worship' originally meant 'worth-ship'. Worship is concerned with the question: What is God worth to me?

Two main things happen in Christian worship:

1 **God comes to us.** God speaks and acts through his Word and Sacraments. He shows us his 'worth' — what a great God he is, especially that he is **for us**.

2 **We respond to God.** We recognize his 'worth'. We praise and thank him for being our great and gracious God. At the same time, we recognize our own unworthiness, confess our sin, and ask him for forgiveness. We also ask him to help us and other people.

Worship is the most important part of our Christian life, because through worship God maintains and strengthens his relationship with us, and the relationship between us and other Christians. We worship God not only in church, but also at home — or wherever we hear or think about his Word and honour him by words and actions.

Photo: The Advertiser.

'Run ... to win the prize,' (1 Corinthians 9:24–27)

BIBLE SEARCH

READ LUKE 10:38–42

What did Jesus mean by the 'one thing' that is needed in our lives?

What do you think of this statement:
'Going to church should not just be a habit, but it is a good habit'.

FULL-TIME PRAYER

Prayer is an important part of our worship-life. God speaks to us in his Word, and we respond in our prayers. Christian prayer is an expression of Christian faith. We pray to God because we know and believe he is **for us**. He is our loving Father who encourages us to pray to him, and who promises to answer in the way that is best for us. The Bible says: **Call upon me in the day of trouble; I will deliver you, and you will honour me'** (Psalm 50:15).

Christian prayer is God's children talking with their Father about things that are important to him and to them. We tell God how much he means to us. We ask him to supply our own and other people's bodily and spiritual needs.

We can pray to the Father as Jesus himself prayed. We pray *in Jesus' name* or *for Jesus' sake*. We can go to our Father in heaven only through Jesus. He listens to us because of Jesus.

In his own way and at his own time, God answers every prayer that is offered in faith. He answers our prayers

    EITHER through something he *says* to us,

    OR through something he *does* to us or for us.

Often God wants to use us as his agents in his answer to prayer. So, for example, when we *pray* for our 'daily bread', we are to realize that God may answer by blessing our daily *work*.

(See the end of the chapter for comments on the Lord's Prayer.)

FULL-TIME WITNESS

Christian commitment includes wanting everyone to know God as their God, and Jesus as their Saviour. We are 'witnesses' of Jesus. We tell other people what we know and believe about him.

As God's children, we are full-time advertisements for our Father. People are able to see what God is like by looking at his children, when we love as he loves, forgive as he forgives, are holy as he is holy.

BIBLE SEARCH

READ **MATTHEW 6:5–15**

Which of Jesus' directions about praying seem most relevant to you?

If God already knows what we need (v 8), why bother to pray?

BIBLE SEARCH

READ **MATTHEW 5:13–16**

Note that Jesus does not say: 'Try to be salt and light'; he says: 'You **are** salt and light'.

How can we act as salt and light... at home?... at work?... in our community involvements?

We can never be perfect witnesses for Jesus. We need his pardon for our failures, and the Holy Spirit's help, so that we can grow in our witnessing.

FULL-TIME SERVICE

Following Jesus means committing ourselves totally to serving him. It means doing what he wants because he is in control of our lives as our Lord and Master.

We can never serve our Lord perfectly. But we trust his mercy to forgive us where we fail. And the more our Father's love fills us, the more we will want to serve him.

Serving God full-time means that every part of our life is sacred; there is no part of our life which is not devoted to God. It means using all our time, abilities, and money to do God's work in the world. This includes:

- ...**working faithfully in our occupation.** Our daily work is not just for making a living, but a way of serving God and other people.

- ...**working faithfully in our congregation and church.** God gives all of us special 'gifts' to be used 'for the common good' (1 Corinthians 12:7).

- ...**carrying out family responsibilities faithfully** (Ephesians 5:21 – 6:4).

- ...**being good citizens:** obeying the laws, paying taxes, working for peace, justice, and the well-being of all (1 Peter 2:13–17).

- ...**helping the poor and needy** (Matthew 25:31–46).

THE LORD'S PRAYER

The Lord's Prayer teaches us a great deal about full-time Christianity.

The Lord's prayer is . . .

- ...**a prayer of disciples.** It can be prayed only by people who believe in Jesus. It is the prayer of God's family.

Jesus gives us a picture of full-time Christianity: 'I am the vine, and you are the branches. Whoever remains in me, and I in him, will bear much fruit; for you can do nothing without me'.
(John 15:5 GNB)

'Our Father, who art in heaven,
Hallowed be thy name.
Thy kingdom come.
Thy will be done on earth as it is in heaven.
Give us this day our daily bread.
And forgive us our trespasses, as we forgive those who trespass against us.
And lead us not into temptation,
But deliver us from evil.
For thine is the kingdom and the power and the glory for ever and ever. Amen.'

...**a confession of faith.** We confess our relationship to God, 'our Father'. He is King, his will is supreme; he forgives, and he provides.

...**a statement of priorities.** Jesus tells us what is important for our lives. He teaches us to put first things first: first, God's concerns, then ours.

...**a framework for all prayer.** Jesus provides the general outline, we are able to fill in the details. Thus, it becomes a new prayer every time we pray it.

...**a prayer of commitment.** We commit ourselves to being God's agents to carry out what we pray for.

...**a prayer of life.** It takes us into every corner of our daily lives. It also takes a lifetime to pray the Lord's Prayer.

THE CHURCH TEACHES
in Luther's *Small Catechism*

The Lord's Prayer

THE INTRODUCTION
Our Father who art in heaven.
What does this mean?
Here God encourages us to believe that he is truly our Father and we are his children. We therefore are to pray to him with complete confidence just as children speak to their loving father.

THE FIRST PETITION
Hallowed be Thy name.
What does this mean?
God's name certainly is holy in itself, but we ask in this prayer that we may keep it holy.
When does this happen?
God's name is hallowed whenever his Word is taught in its truth and purity and we as children of God live in harmony with it. Help us to do this, heavenly Father! But anyone who teaches or lives contrary to the Word of God dishonours God's name among us. Keep us from doing this, heavenly Father!

THE SECOND PETITION
Thy kingdom come.
What does this mean?
God's kingdom comes indeed without our praying for it, but we ask in this prayer that it may come also to us.
When does this happen?
God's kingdom comes when our heavenly Father gives us his Holy Spirit, so that by his grace we believe his holy Word and live a godly life on earth now and in heaven for ever.

NOTES

KEY BIBLE STATEMENTS

- [Jesus said:] No one can serve two masters ... You cannot serve God and Money.
  (Matthew 6:24)

- Let the word of Christ dwell in you richly as you teach and admonish one another with all wisdom, and as you sing psalms, hymns and spiritual songs with gratitude in your hearts to God.
  (Colossians 3:16)

- I urge you ... in view of God's mercy, to offer your bodies as living sacrifices, holy and pleasing to God — which is your spiritual worship.
  (Romans 12:1)

- [Jesus said:] Ask and it will be given to you; seek and you will find; knock and the door will be opened to you.
  (Matthew 7:7)

- [Jesus said:] My Father will give you whatever you ask in my name.
  (John 16:23)

- Whether you eat or drink or whatever you do, do it all for the glory of God.
  (1 Corinthians 10:31)

THE THIRD PETITION
Thy will be done on earth as it is in heaven.
What does this mean?
The good and gracious will of God is surely done without our prayer, but we ask in this prayer that it may be done also among us.
When does this happen?
God's will is done when he hinders and defeats every evil scheme and purpose of the devil, the world, and our sinful self, which would prevent us from keeping his name holy and would oppose the coming of his kingdom. And his will is done when he strengthens our faith and keeps us firm in his Word as long as we live. This is his gracious and good will.

THE FOURTH PETITION
Give us this day our daily bread.
What does this mean?
God gives daily bread, even without our prayer, to all people, though sinful, but we ask in this prayer that he will help us to realize this and to receive our daily bread with thanks.
What is meant by 'daily bread'?
Daily bread includes everything needed for this life, such as food and clothing, home and property, work and income, a devoted family, an orderly community, good government, favourable weather, peace and health, a good name, and true friends and neighbours.

THE FIFTH PETITION
And forgive us our trespasses, as we forgive those who trespass against us.
What does this mean?
We ask in this prayer that our Father in heaven would not hold our sins against us and because of them refuse to hear our prayer. And we pray that he would give us everything by grace, for we sin every day and deserve nothing but punishment. So we on our part will heartily forgive and gladly do good to those who sin against us.

THE SIXTH PETITION
And lead us not into temptation.
What does this mean?
God tempts no one to sin, but we ask in this prayer that God would watch over us and keep us so that the devil, the world, and our sinful self may not deceive us and draw us into false belief, despair, and other great and shameful sins. And we pray that even though we are so tempted we may still win the final victory.

THE SEVENTH PETITION
But deliver us from evil.
What does this mean?
We ask in this inclusive prayer that our heavenly Father would save us from every evil to body and soul, and at our last hour would mercifully take us from the troubles of this world to himself in heaven.

THE DOXOLOGY
For thine is the kingdom and the power and the glory for ever and ever. Amen.
What does 'Amen' mean?
Amen means: Yes, it shall be so. We say Amen because we are certain that such petitions are pleasing to our Father in heaven and are heard by him. For he himself has commanded us to pray in this way and has promised to hear us.

MORE TO THINK ABOUT

1 Think about what this chapter is saying to you personally about full-time Christianity. And does it call for any changes in your ... beliefs? ... attitudes? ... conduct? ... lifestyle?

2 Draw up a reply to the following statements:

'I don't need to go to church. I can worship God just as well at home or out in the country.'

'What I do at work or at home during the week worships and serves God just as much as what I do in church on Sundays.'

3 The next time you go to church, pinpoint those parts of the service in which God is at work, showing us his 'worth', and those parts in which we respond to God.

4 Martin Luther called the Lord's Prayer 'the greatest of martyrs'. Perhaps we *say* the Lord's Prayer too often, and *pray* it too seldom. How can we pray the Lord's Prayer more thoughtfully?

Some suggestions:
- Think of various specific people and needs before you pray.
- Focus on one particular part of the prayer each time. Don't worry if you can't concentrate on every word.

GOD FOR US — FOR EVER!

10

NAME WHICH of the following best describes the way you feel about
a) your own future,
b) the future of our world:

optimistic
excited
afraid
uncertain
confident
hopeful
don't think about it much
pessimistic

LOOKING INTO THE FUTURE

WE TEND to be rather nervous about the future — perhaps even afraid — simply because we don't know what lies ahead, and we are not sure of our own ability to cope.

Actually, the future is God's business, not ours. It's in his hands. He will always be in control. As someone has said:

'We don't know what the future holds,
but we do know who holds the future.'

THE END IS COMING!

Our life on earth is surely coming to an end. But we don't know how much time we will still be given to live on earth.

This world itself is also coming to an end. Since it is ruined and corrupted by sin, God will destroy it some day. But only he knows exactly when and how this will happen.

We don't need to be afraid of either of these ends. Because God is for us, even death can't hurt us. Jesus broke the power of death by his own death and resurrection. For Christians, death is no longer a punishment. When we die, we 'fall asleep in Jesus'. And, for Christians, the end of the world is the day of final deliverance from all evil.

JESUS IS COMING

Before Jesus left his disciples, he told them: **'I am going ... to prepare a place for you. And if I go and prepare a place for you, I will come back and take you to be with me that you also may be where I am'** (John 14:2,3). Ever since, Christians have waited for Jesus' 'second coming' at the end of time.

The same Jesus who once lived and died and rose again as our Saviour — the same Jesus who is invisibly present with us now as our living Lord — will come again in glory. The Bible says: 'This same Jesus, who has been taken from you into heaven, will come back in the same way you have seen him go into heaven' (Acts 1:11).

BIBLE SEARCH

READ **PSALM 23**

Why can we be confident and unafraid as we face the future?

NOTES

BIBLE SEARCH

READ **2 PETER 3:3–15**

Why does God delay the end of the world?

Some people think this world will be destroyed by a nuclear holocaust. How does this idea compare with the prophecy in 2 Peter?

RESURRECTION AND JUDGMENT

When Jesus returns, all people who have ever lived on earth will become alive again. The Creator will give life again to our 'dust and ashes'.

Those who 'fell asleep in Jesus' (died believing in him) will wake again with perfect bodies, free from all sin, suffering, and death. The bodies of Christians who are still living on the Last Day will be transformed.

At the Last Day, Jesus will judge all people who have ever lived. His judgment will show his perfect justice and his amazing grace. The Last Judgment will really be only a public pronouncement of a sentence which is passed on us already in our lifetime: 'Whoever believes in him [Jesus] is not condemned, but whoever does not believe stands condemned already because he has not believed in the name of God's one and only Son' (John 3:18).

When we believe that God is for us, we need not be afraid of the coming judgment. Already now he has declared us 'not guilty' for Jesus' sake.

HEAVEN OR HELL

When Jesus comes to judge the world, those who believe in him will live with him in heaven in perfect happiness for ever. Those who die rejecting God's forgiveness will go to never-ending punishment in hell.

'Heaven' means being with God. 'Hell' means being separated from God. God has not given us all the details about life in heaven. But he does tell us that it will be perfect. The Bible says: 'He will wipe every tear from their eyes. There will be no more death or mourning or crying or pain' (Revelation 21:4).

CAN WE BE SURE?

Can we be sure that we will go to heaven? If we look at ourselves and at our own performance, we have no basis for confidence. But if we look to Jesus, we can be absolutely certain. Because of Jesus, God is **for us now and for ever.** His Word tells us that. Baptism and the Lord's Supper guarantee it.

Through Jesus, the beginning and end of our faith (A and O, Hebrews 12:2), Christians (wheat, Matthew 13:30) have the sure hope of heaven (crown, Revelation 2:10).

BIBLE SEARCH

READ **JOHN 5:24–29**
What good news do you find in these verses?

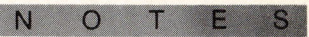

BIBLE SEARCH

READ **REVELATION 7:9–17** for a picture of heaven.

How can we right now experience a taste of heaven?

When we truly believe that God is for us, we can live joyfully and confidently. Whoever believes in Jesus has eternal life right now.

God is for us — for ever! St Paul sums up very beautifully what this means for our future:

'The Lord is my shepherd, I shall lack nothing'.

(Psalm 23:1)

'If God is for us, who can be against us? He who did not spare his own Son, but gave him up for us all — how will he not also, along with him, graciously give us all things? Who will bring any charge against those whom God has chosen? It is God who justifies. Who is he that condemns? Christ Jesus, who died — more than that, who was raised to life — is at the right hand of God and is also interceding for us. Who shall separate us from the love of Christ? Shall trouble or hardship or persecution or famine or nakedness or danger or sword?

As it is written:

'For your sake we face death all day long; We are considered as sheep to be slaughtered.'

No, in all these things we are more than conquerors through him who loved us.

For I am convinced that
neither death nor life,
neither angels nor demons,
neither the present nor the future,
nor any powers,
neither height nor depth,
nor anything else in all creation,
will be able to separate us from the love of God that is in Christ Jesus our Lord.'

Romans 8:31–39

NOTES

KEY BIBLE STATEMENTS

- [Jesus said:] I am the resurrection and the life. He who believes in me will live, even though he dies; and whoever lives and believes in me will never die.
  (John 11:25,26)

- [The Lord Jesus Christ] will transform our lowly bodies so that they will be like his glorious body.
  (Philippians 3:21)

- How great is the love the Father has lavished on us, that we should be called children of God! And that is what we are! ... Now we are children of God, and what we will be has not yet been made known. But we know that when he appears, we shall be like him, for we shall see him as he is.
  (1 John 3:1,2)

- We will be with the Lord for ever.
  (1 Thessalonians 4:17)

- [Jesus said:] Surely I will be with you always, to the very end of the age. (Matthew 28:20)

- [Jesus said:] Be faithful, even to the point of death, and I will give you the crown of life.
  (Revelation 2:10)

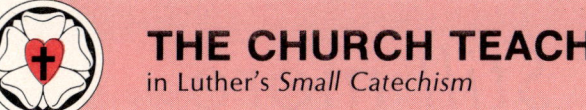

THE CHURCH TEACHES
in Luther's *Small Catechism*

(from The Apostles' Creed)

THE SECOND ARTICLE
And in Jesus Christ, his only Son, our Lord; who was conceived by the Holy Spirit, born of the Virgin Mary; suffered under Pontius Pilate, was crucified, dead, and buried; he descended into hell; the third day he rose again from the dead; he ascended into heaven, and sits at the right hand of God the Father almighty; from thence he will come to judge the living and the dead.
What does this mean?
I believe that Jesus Christ — true God, Son of the Father from eternity, and true man, born of the Virgin Mary — is my Lord.
At great cost he has saved and redeemed me, a lost and condemned person. He has freed me from sin, death, and the power of the devil — not with silver or gold, but with his holy and precious blood and his innocent suffering and death.
All this he has done that I may be his own, live under him in his kingdom, and serve him in everlasting righteousness, innocence, and blessedness, just as he is risen from the dead and lives and rules eternally.
This is most certainly true.

THIRD ARTICLE
In this Christian church day after day he fully forgives my sins and the sins of all believers. On the last day he will raise me and all the dead, and give me and all believers in Christ eternal life.
This is most certainly true.

(from The Lord's Prayer)

THE SEVENTH PETITION
But deliver us from evil.
What does this mean?
We ask in this inclusive prayer that our heavenly Father would save us from every evil to body and soul, and at our last hour would mercifully take us from the troubles of this world to himself in heaven.

MORE TO THINK ABOUT

1 Think about what this chapter is saying to you personally concerning your future. Does this chapter call for changes in your personal ... beliefs? ... attitudes? ... conduct? ... lifestyle?

2 Read 1 Corinthians 15, and note:
- ... how Jesus' resurrection is at the centre of the Christian faith, especially of the belief in our own resurrection;
- ... what kind of bodies we will have when Jesus raises us from death;
- ... what will happen to those still living on the Last Day;
- ... how belief in the resurrection gives us a new outlook on life now.

3 Read Luke 21:5–28. What signs of the end of the world have already happened? What signs still have to happen?

4 Why is it good for us not to know the details about our own future and that of the world? Why don't we need to be afraid even of the possibility of a nuclear war?

Still more to think about!

At the end of each chapter, you have been encouraged to think about what the chapter said to you personally. What changes were called for in your beliefs, attitudes, conduct, lifestyle?

What you have read in this book about 'God for us' looks for a response. What now? Where do you go from here?

Perhaps you now face the question whether or not you will join a church or congregation. Or perhaps you are being called to greater commitment in your present church membership. God will surely guide and bless you in these decisions.

One thing is surely ahead of you — and always will be: the need for your relationship with God to grow stronger and closer. You need to grow in knowing God as your Father and in living as his child.

This book is only an introduction to 'God for us'. Talk with your pastor, or with some other Christian friend, about ongoing opportunities for you to 'grow in the grace and knowledge of our Lord and Saviour Jesus Christ' (2 Peter 3:18).

NOTES

READY REFERENCE

This ready reference lists many important terms referred to in the book, giving a brief explanation or definition where necessary. The listing also includes short explanations of some words and phrases not used in the book, but frequently heard in church.

Absolution: Forgiveness of sins — especially the word of forgiveness spoken to a person who confesses sin and wants to be forgiven. (See ch 8.)

Agnostic: A person who claims that we cannot know for sure whether there is a God or not, and so cannot know anything certain about God.

Angels: Literally means: messengers. Spirits created by God who serve him as messengers, especially by protecting his people. (See ch 4.)

Apostle: Literally means: one who is sent, a messsenger. Jesus' specially-chosen disciples were called apostles.

Ascension: Forty days after Jesus rose from death, he ascended into heaven; he has gone back to his Father to prepare a place for his followers. Jesus now 'sits at the right hand of the Father': he rules together with his Father. (See ch 2.)

Atheist: A person who believes that there is no God.

Atonement: By his death, Jesus atoned or made up for our sins. He paid the penalty for us. (See ch 2.)

Baptism: The Sacrament set up by Jesus. To baptize means to apply water in the name of the Father, Son, and Holy Spirit for forgiveness and salvation. (See ch 5.)

Bible: Literally means: book. Also called Holy Scripture (= holy writing). A library of 66 books written over a period of approximately 1500 years by men whom God inspired. (See ch 3.)

Bless: To bless a person means to pronounce God's favour on someone, resulting in happiness and prosperity. To bless God means to adore God and say how good he is.

Born again: Everyone who believes in Jesus and is baptized in the name of the Father, Son, and Holy Spirit is 're-born' as a child of God, begins a new life as a new person, with a new nature. The Holy Spirit works this miracle through the Gospel (good news) of Jesus. (See ch 5, 6.)

Catechism: A book of instruction using questions and answers. Martin Luther wrote two catechisms (the *Small Catechism* and the *Large Catechism*). These are accepted by Lutherans as correct statements of their teaching, based on the Bible.

Catholic: Literally means: universal, or world-wide. Lutherans believe in 'the holy catholic Church'. (See ch 8.) The phrase 'the holy Christian Church' is used in the Creed to avoid confusion with 'the Roman Catholic Church'.

Church: See ch 8.

Christ: Jesus' title. Literally means: the anointed one, one set apart for a special task ('Messiah' in the Old Testament). Jesus was anointed to be our Prophet, Priest, and King.

Communion/communicant: A communicant is a person who receives Communion (or Holy Communion). (See ch 7.) **First Communion:** Usually, children receive Communion for the first time when they are confirmed. However, some Lutheran churches admit children to Communion before they are confirmed, but after they indicate their wish to commune and have received proper instruction.

Confession: (a) Admitting our sin. We confess our sins publicly in the church service. We may also privately confess to a pastor or other fellow-Christian particular sins that are on our conscience.

(b) A statement of beliefs and teachings. The Lutheran 'Confessions' were written at the time of the Reformation. They are accepted by most Lutherans as correct explanations of the teachings of the Bible. The main confessions are: the Augsburg Confession; Luther's Small Catechism; Luther's Large Catechism.

Confirmation: A church ceremony in which people who have been instructed in the Christian/Lutheran faith publicly confess their faith and their intention to continue in the faith. Usually they receive Holy Communion for the first time when they are confirmed. (See **Communion** above.)

Congregation: A local gathering of Christians who come together for worship. In the Lutheran Church, each congregation has the authority to make its own decisions, but is encouraged to bear in mind the welfare of the Church as a whole. (See ch 8.)

Conscience: An inner sense of right and wrong. Since the Fall into sin, the human conscience is unreliable unless it is guided by the Word of God.

Conversion: To be converted means to be turned from unbelief to faith. We can't convert ourselves by making our own 'decision for Christ'. It is the Holy Spirit who converts people by leading them to faith in Jesus as their Saviour. (See ch 3,5,6.)

Covenant: A treaty, pact, or contract. In the Bible, the term refers to an agreement God makes with people, promising to be their God and to bless them (e.g., in Baptism; see ch 5).

Creation: To create means to bring into existence, to make out of nothing. (See ch 4.)

Creed: A statement of belief. The three 'ecumenical' (accepted by the major Christian churches) creeds are: The Apostles' Creed; The Nicene Creed; The Athanasian Creed. The creeds are used in Lutheran church services as common statements of faith.

Death: Separation. Physical death is separation from the body. Spiritual death is separation from God in this life. Eternal death is the never-ending separation from God in hell.

Denomination: A group of Christians and/or congregations which has specific beliefs, teachings, and practices. (See ch 8.)

Devil: The enemy of God, of human beings, and of all that is good. Also called Satan. Originally a holy angel, the devil rebelled against God and was banished to hell (2 Peter 2:4). The devil is the 'tempter' who tries to lead us into sin. (See ch 4.)

Disciple: A follower of Jesus. Every Christian is a disciple (= learner), who is called to follow Jesus and to learn from him.

Discipline: If a member of a congregation falls into some sin, and it is obvious that he/she does not repent, it is the duty of the other members lovingly to warn and correct that person. This is called 'church discipline' (Matthew 18:15-18; Galatians 6:1).

Doctrine: A teaching of the Bible, or of a denomination (for example, the doctrine of Creation).

Doxology: A song of praise to God.

Elders: In the Lutheran Church, elders are laymen elected by a congregation to help the pastor(s) care for the members of the congregation.

End of the World:	See ch 10.
Eschatology:	The Bible's teachings about the last things (the end of the world, Jesus' second coming, etc.). (See ch 10.)
Eternal:	Timeless, never-ending. God is eternal — without beginning or end. All who believe in Jesus as their Saviour have God's free gift of eternal life with him.
Evangelism:	Evangel means Gospel, the good news of Jesus. Evangelism is communicating the good news of Jesus, especially to people who are not Christians. (See ch 9.)
Excommunication:	The excluding from a congregation of a person who obviously will not repent of some sin, even though he/she has been urged to do so (as Jesus directed in Matthew 18:15–18; see **Discipline** above). A congregation takes this step only as a last resort in the attempt to lead the person to turn away from sin and to receive God's forgiveness.
Faith:	(a) Belief or trust — especially putting our confidence or trust in Jesus as our only Saviour. Faith is not a decision we make by our own willpower; it is a gift of the Holy Spirit. (See ch 2,3,6.)
	(b) Faith can also mean a set of beliefs, what is believed and taught in the Church. (e.g., We have learnt the Christian 'faith' from this book.)
Fall:	When the first human beings disobeyed God, they 'fell' from the perfect state in which God had created them. The Fall into sin ruined God's whole creation. Our sinful nature is a product of the Fall. (See ch 4.)
Fellowship:	Christian fellowship means belonging to the family of God with other Christians, and enjoying oneness in Christ.
Flesh:	The term often used in the Bible for the sinful human nature with which we are born. (See ch 1,4,6.)
Forgiveness:	To forgive means to let someone go free of the guilt and punishment he/she has deserved, not to hold against a person the wrong he/she has done. Jesus won God's forgiveness for all people; everyone who believes in him has the forgiveness of all sins. (See ch 2.)
Freedom/liberty:	Christians have been set free by Jesus from the demands of God's Law, from the guilt, punishment, and power of sin. We have been set free to be God's holy people; we are free to gladly serve him and other people. 'Christian liberty' also means that we are free to make our own decisions in all matters where God has given us no specific instructions (cf Romans 14:1–8; Galatians 5:1). (See ch 6.)
Gentiles:	In the Old Testament, all nations apart from God's chosen people, Israel, were called Gentiles. The word is sometimes widened to mean unbelievers.
Gospel:	(a) The main truth of the Bible. The good news that God loves all people despite their sin; that Jesus is the Saviour of all because he gave his life for all; and that all who believe in Jesus have the free gift of everlasting life. (See ch 2,3, etc.)
	(b) The first four books of the New Testament are called gospels because they recount the life, death, and resurrection of Jesus our Saviour.
Grace:	The undeserved love of God for us. God accepts and forgives sinners 'by grace', moved by his own love. (See ch 2, etc.)
Heaven:	Where God is. Because heaven is beyond our dimensions of time and space, the Bible often uses picture-language to describe it (e.g., a city of gold). To be in heaven means to be with God. (See ch 10.)
Hell:	The opposite of heaven. The state of never-ending separation from God. The Bible uses the picture of 'hell-fire' to describe the agony of being cut off from God. (See ch 10.)

Holy:	Separate or set apart. God is 'holy' because he is set apart from all other beings as the perfect, sinless One. Christians are holy in God's sight because Jesus has taken their sin on himself.
Holy Communion:	One of God's means of grace (see ch 6). Other names are: The Sacrament of the Altar; The Lord's Supper; The Eucharist (= Thanksgiving); The Lord's Table. 'Communion' means fellowship, belonging together, sharing together. (See ch 7.)
Holy Spirit:	The Third Person in the Holy Trinity, true God, together with the Father and the Son. The Spirit's special work is to make people holy by bringing them to faith in Jesus and giving them new life as God's children. After people become Christians, the Holy Spirit maintains and strengthens faith through the means of grace. (See ch 3,5,6,8.)
Idolatry:	Having a false god. We commit idolatry if we fear, love, and trust anyone or anything more than God (see the First Commandment).
Image of God:	God made human beings holy and immortal like himself (Genesis 1:26); they fell from this original condition when they sinned. The Holy Spirit re-creates people in God's image when he brings them to faith in Jesus (Ephesians 4:24). The image of God also includes mankind's ability to reason, to make decisions of right and wrong, and to relate to God through worship. (See ch 4.)
Incarnation:	Literally means: becoming flesh. Jesus, the eternal Son of God, became a true human being when he was born of the Virgin Mary. Jesus is 'God incarnate', God and man in one person. (See ch 2.)
Infant Baptism:	See ch 5.
Inherited Sin (original sin):	The sin passed on from sinful parents to their children. Since the Fall into sin, all human beings are born with inherited sin, and need God's grace. (See ch 1,5.)
Inspiration:	To inspire means to breathe into. The Holy Spirit inspired men to write down God's Word in the Bible. (See ch 3.)
Intercession:	A form of prayer. To intercede means to pray for someone else.
Jesus:	Means 'Saviour'. (See ch 2, etc.)
Judgment:	God is the supreme Judge of all people. All people deserve to be found guilty under God's judgment, but God put Jesus on trial instead of us. Since Jesus was found guilty and sentenced to death for us, all who believe in Jesus have already survived God's judgment. **Judgment Day:** The final judgment at the end of the world, when God's judgment on all people will be pronounced according to their response to God's grace. (See ch 10.)
Justification:	To justify means to declare not guilty. Because of Jesus' death on the cross for and in the place of the whole human race, God declares all people not guilty. He offers his forgiveness to all as a free gift. Everyone who by the power of the Holy Spirit accepts God's offer is forgiven.
Keys (Office of the Keys):	The power Jesus has given his followers to open or close heaven to people by forgiving or retaining (not forgiving) their sins. (See ch 8.)
Kingdom of God:	God's rule over people as Creator, Redeemer, and Sanctifier. God rules not only with power and majesty, but also especially with his grace. He sets up his rule over people through the Gospel of Jesus (including the Sacraments), by which the Holy Spirit works trust in God and his grace.
Law:	One of the main teachings of the Bible. Tells us what God demands, and threatens to punish disobedience. The Law always condemns us because we can't obey it. But Jesus obeyed the Law for us, and paid for our lawbreaking on the cross. All who trust Jesus are free from the Law's demands and

	threats. However, believers in Jesus also learn from the Law what the life of a disciple involves. (See ch 1,3,6.)
Layman/laywoman/ layperson/laity:	A lay person is a member of the Church who is not a clergyman. In some churches, 'lay workers' are employed for particular ministry duties. Lutherans use layreaders, but usually not lay preachers.
Liturgy:	A form of public worship. The Lutheran Church is 'liturgical'; it uses a set order of service rather than 'free' forms of worship. Lutheran liturgies usually draw on traditions passed down over many centuries. See Appendix page 61.
Lutheran:	Originally a nickname given to followers of Martin Luther, the Protestant reformer. 'Lutherans' share Martin Luther's understanding of the main teachings of the Bible.
Means of Grace:	The 'channels' the Holy Spirit uses to bring us God's love: the Word of God and the Sacraments (Baptism and Holy Communion). (See ch 3,5,6,7,8.)
Mercy:	Pity, sympathy, kindness toward people who have not deserved it. God is merciful to us, and tells us to be merciful to others.
Messiah:	Hebrew equivalent of the Greek name *Christ*. See **Christ** above.
Ministry:	Literally means: service. All Christians are called to minister by serving God and other people in their daily work and with their talents. The **Office of the (Public) Ministry** is the specific work of publicly preaching and teaching God's Word to which pastors are called. An alternative title for pastors is ministers (= servants).
Mission:	Literally means: sending. Jesus sends all his followers out to their own community and nation, and then to all nations, as 'missionaries of the Gospel'. The term 'missionary' is usually applied to professional Christian workers sent by the Church to work among non-Christians.
Natural Knowledge of God:	See ch 3.
Neighbour:	Every other human being, especially those who need our help. (See ch 1.)
New Birth:	See **Born Again** above.
New Testament:	(a) The 27 books of the Bible written since the incarnation of Jesus Christ.
	(b) The term is also used to describe God's grace and forgiveness for all people through Christ's life, death, and resurrection. In Holy Communion, Christ gives us his 'blood of the new testament [covenant]'.
Offence:	In the biblical sense, anything which causes someone to stumble spiritually.
Ordination:	The church ceremony by which qualified persons are publicly declared to be ministers of Christ, authorized to preach, baptize, and administer Holy Communion.
Original Sin:	See **Inherited Sin** above.
Parables:	Stories from nature and life which Jesus told to teach people about God and his rule.
Passion:	The 'Passion of our Lord' means the suffering of Jesus leading up to and including his death on the cross as our Saviour.
Pastor:	Literally means: shepherd. The title given by Lutherans to a person called by a congregation to 'feed and lead' its members by carrying out the Office of the Ministry. (See ch 8.)
Prayer:	See ch 9.

Prophet:	A person whom God called and inspired to speak his divine word of judgment and/or promise. This sometimes included predicting future events.
Propitiation:	See **Atonement** above.
Providence:	God our Father's care for his creation. He provides us with what we need. He makes all things work for good for his children. (See ch 4.)
Real Presence:	In Holy Communion, the body and blood of Jesus are actually present with the bread and wine. All communicants receive Christ's true body, given into death, and Christ's true blood, shed on the cross for sin.
Reconciliation:	The removal of the barrier between God and human beings caused by sin. We are reconciled to God when faith grasps the forgiveness earned by Christ on the cross. Christians living in that forgiveness then work for reconciliation between people.
Redemption:	God's act of buying back sinful humanity. Jesus bought us back from sin, death, and the power of the devil; it cost him his life to redeem us. (See ch 2.)
Reformation:	The movement in the 16th century to correct unbiblical teaching and practice in the church of that day. Martin Luther was the leading reformer. See Appendix page 63.
Regeneration:	Re-birth and the gift of spiritual life. See **Born Again** and **Conversion** above.
Renewal:	Being made new again. The Holy Spirit makes people new when he brings them to faith in Christ (for example, through Baptism). He renews us again and again by calling us to repentance, stronger faith, and God-pleasing living. Through God's Word and Sacraments, he helps us 'put off' the old nature and 'put on' the new nature. (See ch 5,6.)
Repentance:	The change of heart brought about by the Holy Spirit through God's Word. It includes both turning away from sin and turning in faith to God for forgiveness. (See ch 3,5,6.)
Resurrection:	God's act of bringing back to life again those who have died. Jesus' resurrection has made it certain that all believers will be raised from death on the Last Day to enjoy eternal life with Christ. (See ch 2,10.)
Revelation:	To reveal means to make known. God has revealed himself in various ways, especially through the Bible (God's written revelation) and through Jesus Christ (the Word incarnate). (See ch 3, and **Word of God** below.)
Righteousness:	To be righteous means to be right, good, innocent. God is righteous, and expects us to be righteous, too. Righteousness — being right with God — comes not by our performance or achievements, but only by faith in Jesus. Because Jesus took our place, God credits Jesus' righteousness to all who trust in him. See **Justification** above. (See ch 2.)
Right Hand of God:	God's action in carrying out his purposes. The risen and ascended Jesus 'sits at God's right hand': rules over all things for the good of his Church.
Sacred:	Holy, set apart for God.
Sacrament:	The Lutheran Church defines a sacrament as a holy act commanded by God, in which earthly elements are used with God's Word to pass on to us God's grace and blessing. (See ch 5,6.) Christ gave us two sacraments: Holy Baptism, and Holy Communion.
Saint:	Holy person. All who believe in Jesus as their Saviour are saints, or holy people, because they have the forgiveness of their sins. (See ch 8.)

Salvation:	Being saved (made safe) from sin and its consequences. The work Jesus did for us as our *Saviour*. Sometimes it refers to our final deliverance when we are 'safe and sound' in heaven for ever. Salvation is God's free gift, which he offers to us through his Word and Sacraments. (See ch 2,5,7,10.)
Sanctification:	To sanctify means to make separate, to make holy. The Holy Spirit sanctifies us by making our lives holy. While we become God's children in the instant we come to faith in Jesus, our growing in holiness is an on-going process. We will reach perfection only in heaven. (See ch 6.)
Saviour:	One who saves, rescues, delivers. The name Jesus means Saviour. He has saved or rescued us from sin, death, hell, and the power of the devil. (See ch 2.)
Scripture:	See **Bible** above.
Second Coming:	Jesus' return in glory for the final judgment at the end of the world. No one knows the date of the Second Coming. The Bible urges us to be ready for it all the time. (See ch 10.)
Sin:	Anything that separates us from God. It includes the evil nature we inherit, and our breaking God's Law by doing what we shouldn't, or not doing what we should. Other words for sin are: trespass, transgression, lawlessness, debt. (See ch 1,5.)
Soul:	The non-physical part of a person; the essence of the life God gave to human beings.
Sponsors:	Godparents. Persons who make themselves responsible for infants presented for Baptism. Sponsors witness the baptism, pray for the child, and assist parents in the Christian upbringing of the child.
Stewardship:	In the Bible, a steward is a manager, caretaker, or trustee. We belong to God with all we are and have — our time, abilities, money, possessions, etc. Moved by God's grace toward us, we want to serve him with everything he has entrusted to us. (See ch 9.)
Temptation:	To tempt means to put to the test. God uses times of testing to bring or keep us close to him. The devil, the world (people opposed to God), and our own sinful flesh try to lead us away from God. (See ch 6.)
Theology:	The study of God and of his revelation to humankind; a set of teachings about God.
Trinity/Triune:	Church terms to describe the truth that the true God is Father, Son, and Holy Spirit — three distinct Persons in one God. The term does not occur in the Bible, but is supported by many Scripture passages. (See ch 3,5.)
Virgin Birth:	The Bible teaching that Jesus' mother, Mary, was a virgin. Jesus was conceived by the Holy Spirit's power, not by human sexual union. (See ch 2.)
Will of God:	What God wants to do for us — especially his desire to save us. Also what God wants us to do, and to experience. In situations where we do not know exactly what God wants for us, we pray: 'If it is your will, Lord'.
Word of God:	God's revealing of himself to human beings. The Bible calls Jesus the Word [of God] in John 1 because he revealed God's grace and truth to us in his incarnation. The Bible also calls itself the Word of God because it is God's message to us through inspired human writers. (See ch 2,3.)
Worship:	A public or private act by which God comes to us with his grace through Word and Sacraments, and we respond in prayer, praise, and thanksgiving. (See ch 9.)

THE CHURCH YEAR

The Christian Church has a long-standing tradition of using a calendar of special days and seasons to help worshippers focus on the central truths of Christianity. Each Sunday, festival day, and season of the church year has a special message for us.

A 'liturgical colour' is often used to symbolize the message of a particular day or season.

Advent: Four Sundays before Christmas. (Advent means 'coming'.) A season of preparation for the coming of Christ. A time of repentance and of hope.

Colour: Violet, the colour of royalty, but also a symbol of repentance; or Blue, the colour of hope.

Christmas: The celebration of the birth of Jesus our Saviour. Begins on Christmas Eve, and lasts for 12 days to January 6, including Christmas Day on December 25.

Colour: White, the colour of perfection, light, glory, purity, symbolizing the purity of our Lord.

Epiphany: The Epiphany is celebrated on January 6, and is followed by a post-Epiphany season of from one to nine Sundays, depending on the date of Easter. The Epiphany message stresses that Jesus was revealed as God's Son and the Saviour of all people.

Colour: White for Epiphany and the Sunday following. Green, symbolizing life and growth, for the post-Epiphany season. White for the last Sunday after Epiphany, celebrating the Transfiguration.

Lent: Approximately six weeks from Ash Wednesday to Holy Saturday. A season of repentance, as we remember the suffering and death of Jesus, our Saviour. Lent ends with Holy Week, which includes Maundy Thursday (the day on which Jesus gave the Lord's Supper) and Good Friday (the day on which Jesus died).

Colour: Violet, symbolizing repentance. White on Maundy Thursday. Black on Good Friday (the colour of darkness, the absence of light, symbolizing death and deep sorrow).

Easter Day: The day of Jesus' resurrection. The Easter season lasts for 40 days, until Ascension Day, when Jesus returned to his Father in heaven.

Colour: White.

Pentecost: 50 days after Easter, the day when the Holy Spirit came to Jesus' disciples; the birthday of the Christian Church.

Colour: Red, the colour of blood and fire. Red is often used on days which mark great events in the work of the Christian Church.

The first Sunday after Pentecost is Holy Trinity Sunday. Colour: White.

Post-Pentecost Season: Between 22 and 28 Sundays after Pentecost. The general theme of the non-festival part of the church year is growth in Christian faith and life.

Colour: Green.

A LOOK AT LITURGY

Lutherans usually follow a 'liturgy' or fixed order of worship in their church services. Some of the reasons why Lutherans use a 'liturgical' form of worship are:

> A carefully-designed order of worship helps to make sure that proper balance and emphasis is given to the most important elements of worship — God's coming to us through Word and Sacraments, and our response to him. A good liturgy lessens the chances that worshippers will concentrate more on their performance than on God's coming to serve them.
>
> A common liturgy helps to unite the congregation with fellow-worshippers everywhere.
>
> Lutheran liturgy is traditional; it has been passed down from previous generations of Christians. Using a traditional liturgy helps us realize that we belong to the Christian church of all ages.

Liturgy, however, can also have some disadvantages. It can easily become just a ritual which worshippers rush through without thinking. It is important that worshippers understand the liturgy, so that they can use it as an aid to genuine worship.

A BRIEF EXPLANATION OF THE LITURGY

There are two 'high points' in the Lutheran Service With Holy Communion: when God speaks to us in his Word, and when God serves us with his Sacrament. The liturgy is built around these high points, helping us to prepare ourselves for God's coming to us, and then to respond to his service.

Some parts of the liturgy are the same every Sunday. These are called the 'ordinary' or regular parts. Other parts change from Sunday to Sunday to stress the main theme of worship for that day. These changing parts are called the 'propers' or distinctive parts.

The Invocation

We come together in the name of the Triune God, the name into which we were baptized. We belong to him; we are his children. We are now in his presence, for he is present where his Word is proclaimed and his Sacraments are administered.

Confession and Absolution

How shall we appear before God? As we begin our worship, we remember that we are sinners, that we do not deserve any good thing from God. After we confess our sins, we receive his pardon (Absolution).

Having God's word of forgiveness, we now begin the main part of the service with a Psalm or a selection of verses called the Introit (= entrance), setting the tone for the day's worship.

The Kyrie (Lord, have mercy)

We recognize God as the almighty King who is coming to us. We ask him to show us mercy and to help us in our need.

The Hymn of Praise

In song we glorify God who has revealed himself in Jesus Christ. The hymn may be either the ancient Glory to God in the Highest (which begins with the song of the Christmas angels) or the This Is the Feast/Worthy Is Christ (which draws from various hymns in Revelation).

The Greeting

Minister and congregation in turn greet each other, asking God to give his blessing to them as his Word is read and proclaimed.

The Collect

We pray, 'collecting' the thoughts of the day into one short prayer or collect.

The Readings From Scripture

Our Father serves us, his children. He speaks his holy Word to us in Bible readings from the Old Testament, the letters in the New Testament, and the Gospels (the story of Jesus). We stand for the reading of the Gospel as a mark of respect for our Lord.

The Creed	With the Church of all ages, we respond to the Word of life by our confession of faith in the Triune God. Using one of the Creeds, we tell one another and the whole world what we believe about God. Sometimes the Creed is said after the sermon.
The Sermon	Again our Father serves us, his children, through his Word as the minister preaches. The sermon is to build us up in our faith and to motivate us for our lives as God's children.
The Offertory	In response to God's message, we make our thankofferings to him and dedicate ourselves to him.
The Prayer Of The Church	We pray the Prayer of the Church, which is a prayer for the whole church and all people, but which may also include special requests for individual needs. This general prayer is like a framework for the prayers of each worshipper.
	(If Holy Communion is not being celebrated, the service concludes with the Lord's Prayer, and the Blessing at this point.)
HOLY COMMUNION	God serves us again now with the very best of his gifts: the body and blood of his own dear Son, which were given and shed for the forgiveness of our sins.
The Preface **The Sanctus** (Holy Holy Holy)	We prepare to receive the Sacrament of the Altar with sentences of joy and thanksgiving, and join with saints and angels in praising our Saviour ('Holy, holy, holy … ')
The Lord's Prayer	We pray the Lord's Prayer as a summary of the blessings we seek from our Father.
Words Of Institution	The minister reads the Words of Institution. The Word of God, used with the bread and wine, makes this sacrament a 'means of grace'.
The Lamb of God (Agnus Dei)	Our response of faith is a simple prayer to Christ, the Lamb of God, who offered himself as the perfect sacrifice for the sins of the world.
	The communicants come to the altar and kneel. With the bread and wine they receive Christ's true body and blood 'given and shed for the forgiveness of sins'.
The Song Of Simeon (Nunc Dimittis)	Jesus has come to us, assuring us of his forgiveness, peace, and presence among us. We respond with the Song of Simeon from Luke 2:29–32 (or another post-communion song), followed by the sentences and prayer of thanksgiving.
The Blessing	The service concludes with a word of blessing. This is not a prayer, but a pronouncement. God assures us that he will go with us as our gracious God to guard and help us and give us his peace.

A BRIEF HISTORICAL BACKGROUND

The Lutheran Church, the oldest and largest Protestant church in the world, came into existence through the Reformation in the 16th century AD. However, Lutherans believe and maintain that the teachings of the Lutheran Church give it continuity right back to the apostles and to the Lord Jesus himself.

The Christian church has had many ups and downs throughout its history. There have been times of rapid growth, and times of numerical decline. There have been times when obviously the Holy Spirit was powerfully at work in the hearts and lives of people, and other times when the church seemed completely stagnant. There have been times of peace and quietness, and also times of persecution, when powerful enemies of the church have hounded Christians, put them in prison, tortured or killed them because they confessed Jesus Christ as their only Lord. However, far from destroying the church, persecution often strengthened the commitment of those who were Christians.

Again and again the church has experienced division. A notable example was the major split in 1054 AD when Christians were divided into the Roman Catholic Church (in the west) and the Greek Orthodox Church (in the east). Every generation of Christians has had to cope with false teachers in the church and with arguments about the interpretation of the Bible.

So, the history of the Christian church has been a story of human weakness and sin, but at the same time it is the story of God's grace and faithfulness. The Lord has marvellously fulfilled his promise that not even 'the gates of hell' would overcome his church (Matthew 16:18); he has revived his church when it seemed lifeless, and reformed it when it became corrupt.

Martin Luther:

Martin Luther was one person through whom God reformed the church. When Luther was born in Germany in 1483, the Roman Catholic Church was in bad shape. For years it had been plagued by corrupt and inept leaders — priests, bishops, even popes. There was much religious ignorance and superstition. Few church-members knew much about the Bible; pronouncements by the church and its leaders were held up before the people as the supreme authority. The Gospel of God's forgiveness as a free gift, which is ours only through faith in Jesus, was largely forgotten and seldom proclaimed. Instead, people were encouraged to rely on their own good works and religious performances to get right with God.

Luther, too, was brought up to think of God as an angry judge who was waiting to punish him for his sins. As a spiritually-earnest young man, Luther decided to become a monk; he believed that, if he led a good religious life, he would make himself acceptable to God. But he found no peace; his sins continued to torment him constantly.

Good News for Luther:

The church soon ordained Luther as a priest, and later made him a Doctor of Theology. While studying and lecturing on the Bible (especially the Epistle to the Romans), Luther came to realize that a good standing before God does not depend on our own efforts, but is due entirely to God's mercy shown to us through Jesus. We are saved not by works, but by grace alone, through faith in Jesus Christ. Luther had discovered the good news that God is for us for Jesus' sake.

Luther did not set out to split or undermine the church, but he could not keep quiet about the things he had learnt from the Bible. On October 31, 1517, he posted on the door of the castle church at Wittenberg 95 Theses (statements for debate), questioning some of the church's teachings and practices — especially the selling of 'indulgences' as payment for sins. The common people welcomed the Theses so enthusiastically that the church leaders felt compelled to take action, lest their authority be undermined. Luther was accused of heresy (false teaching), and summoned before various gatherings of leaders of the church. When Luther resisted the papal threats, and kept on questioning teachings and practices of the church, the pope responded by excommunicating him in early 1521.

Later that year, Emperor Charles V, pressed to match the church's action with a political ban, summoned Luther to Worms to answer charges of false teaching. Luther refused to take back what he had written unless he could be shown from the Bible that he was wrong; the Holy Scriptures, he maintained, are our supreme authority.

Duly placed under the Emperor's ban, Luther was in danger of being killed as an outlaw, but friends 'kidnapped' him and took him into hiding in the Wartburg castle. He spent some of his time of seclusion translating the Bible into German so that ordinary people could (for the first time) read God's Word for themselves. Eventually, Luther felt compelled to come out of hiding and to resume his public preaching in order to restrain some of the radical reformers who wanted to sweep away almost anything connected with Roman Catholicism.

Luther broke with a church tradition when he married a former nun, Katharina von Bora. Six children were born to them, and their home was noted for its generous hospitality. Luther's writings stressed the importance of family life, especially the role of fathers in the Christian education of their children.

The Lutheran Church: In 1530, the 'Lutherans' (as Luther's followers had been nicknamed) prepared a statement of their teachings for presentation to a meeting of leaders of church and state at Augsburg. This statement — now known as the Augsburg Confession — became the first official 'confession' or doctrinal statement of the Lutheran Church. Fifty years later, all the confessions of the Lutheran Church were published in the Book of Concord. These are: the Apostles' Creed, the Nicene Creed, the Athanasian Creed, the Augsburg Confession, the Apology (Defence) of the Augsburg Confession, the Smalcald Articles, the Small Catechism and the Large Catechism of Luther, and the Formula of Concord.

By the time Luther died in 1546, the Lutheran Reformation had spread through much of Europe, especially the Scandinavian and Baltic countries, as well as Germany. Political events prevented the Lutheran Church from establishing itself in the British Isles, but Luther's teachings greatly influenced the Protestant Reformation in both England and Scotland.

Lutheran missionaries have taken the Gospel of Christ to most countries of the world. The Lutheran Church was brought to other countries such as USA, Canada, and Australia by immigrants from Europe, some of whom left their homeland seeking freedom of worship.

The main areas of Lutheran population today are Germany, Scandinavia, USA, and Africa. The fastest-growing Lutheran churches in the world today are in Third World countries — especially in Africa.

FOR FURTHER READING

Recommended books for further study of Lutheran teachings include:

Luther's Large Catechism. Available in an excellent, contemporary translation by F.Hebart (published by Lutheran Publishing House, Adelaide, SA).

The Augsburg Confession. Available from all Lutheran publishing houses.

The Book of Concord. The Confessions of the Evangelical Lutheran Church. Translated and edited by T.G. Tappert (Fortress Press, Philadelphia).

One in the Gospel. A popular commentary on the last of the Lutheran Confessions, by F. Hebart (Lutheran Publishing House, Adelaide, SA and Concordia Publishing House, St Louis).

Growing as God's People. A confirmation class learning resource based on Luther's Small Catechism (Lutheran Publishing House, Adelaide, SA).

Masterplan. An overview of God's plan revealed in the Bible, by V.C. Pfitzner (Lutheran Publishing House, Adelaide, SA).